200

DISHES

200

HAMLYN **ALL COLOUR COOKBOOK**

TAPAS & SPANISH DISHES

EMMA LEWIS

An Hachette UK company
www.hachette.co.uk

First published in Great Britain in 2013 by Hamlyn,
a division of Octopus Publishing Group Ltd
Carmelite House, 50 Victoria Embankment
London EC4Y 0DZ
www.octopusbooks.co.uk

This edition published in 2016

ISBN 978-0-600-63336-5

A CIP catalogue record for this book is available
from the British Library

Printed and bound in China

10 9 8 7

Standard level spoon measurement are used in all recipes.
1 tablespoon = one 15 ml spoon
1 teaspoon = one 5 ml spoon

Both imperial and metric measurements have been given in all
recipes. Use one set of measurements only and not a mixture
of both.

Fresh herbs should be used unless otherwise stated.

Eggs should be medium unless otherwise stated. The
Department of Health advises that eggs should not be
consumed raw. This book contains dishes made with raw
or lightly cooked eggs. It is prudent for more vulnerable
people such as pregnant and nursing mothers, invalids,
the elderly, babies and young children to avoid uncooked
or lightly cooked dishes made with eggs. Once prepared
these dishes should be kept refrigerated and used promptly.

Ovens should be preheated to the specific temperature – if
using a fan-assisted oven, follow manufacturer's instructions
for adjusting the time and the temperature.

This book includes dishes made with nuts and nut derivatives.
It is advisable for customers with known allergic reactions to
nuts and nut derivatives to check the labels of pre-prepared
ingredients for the possible inclusion of nut derivatives.

contents

introduction

introduction

Spain is a vast collection of different regions –
from bustling coastal cities to the huge lonely
plains of the interior. Many people have
passed through and left a mark on the cuisine.
The ancient Celts contributed a love of pork,
the Romans introduced the mighty olive
and the Arabs gave a hint of exoticism with
spices and citrus fruits. More recently, Spain
has been setting the trend for foodies all
over the world with its passion for molecular
gastronomy, a style of cooking where science

meets the kitchen stove. Traditional Spanish
food, like so many Mediterranean diets, has
become more popular in recent years with its
focus on fish, vegetables, pulses and olive oil.
But the real joy of Spanish food probably lies
with the laid-back Spanish lifestyle. Evening
meals often start late. To compensate, bars
traditionally served a snack or tapa for people
to nibble on with a drink before the main
event. Before long these became a meal in
their own right, a great opportunity to gather a
group of people and share a variety of dishes,
taking a little taste from each one. It's an easy,
convivial way of eating. This book can be used
to cook up a complete feast of tapas dishes,
one or two only before trying a main course or
just for a quick snack.

the spanish larder

Cheeses

The Spanish don't usually eat a cheese
course, preferring to simply serve a cheese
with some raisins or membrillo, a quince paste,
as a tapa or the rural favourite of drizzling
honey over. Traditional cheesemaking, which
was neglected for many years, is witnessing a
revival with sheeps' and goats' cheese being
especial favourites. Manchego cheese, which
is widely available, is a sheeps' cheese with a
buttery and not too strong flavour.

Hams

Spanish ham is growing in popularity and
the most common variety is Serrano ham.

thickening and giving extra flavour to savoury dishes. Look out especially for Marcona almonds, a traditional Spanish variety that is rounder and sweeter than ordinary ones.

Olives

Olives make a great snack to nibble on while preparing a meal. In Spain, they are often served stuffed with some garlic, pepper and anchovy or even a whole almond. Large green Manzanilla olives are a good choice, as are the small purplish Arbequina olives from Catalonia. It's best to avoid canned, ready-pitted olives, as they tend to lose much of their flavour.

Similar to Italian Parma ham, which can be used as a substitute, it is a dry-cured ham with a full flavour and can be eaten raw as well as used for cooking. Less common and more expensive is Ibérico ham. This ham is produced from the dark Ibérico pig and the best variety – Jamón Ibérico de Bellota – is made from pigs reared on acorns. Its rich flavour makes it much sought after, and it's best to enjoy it simply with, perhaps, a glass of wine.

Nuts

Nuts are an important part of Spanish cooking. You'll find them roasted or fried and simply served as a snack, made into pastes and cakes for dessert and used in sauces for

Olive oil

Olive groves thrive all over Spain and the country is the biggest exporter of olive oil in the world. It is the basis of many dishes and essential to cooking Spanish food. There are a number of specialist olive oil producers whose oil rivals the best found in Italy. But extra virgin olive oil is best saved for finishing dishes and dressing salads. Regular olive oil should be used for frying or when large amounts are needed.

Peppers

You'll find peppers in many Spanish dishes, although this shouldn't put you off if you don't like spicy food, as recipes are often made using peppers with milder flavours. Increasingly, more specialist peppers are available outside of the country. Look out for Padrón peppers – usually mild but the occasional one is extremely hot. Tiny piquillo peppers can sometimes be bought roasted or stuffed and preserved in jars.

Pimentón

Ground pepper is known as pimentón and is used in all types of Spanish cooking. It can be smoked before being ground, which gives an unusual extra flavour to a finished dish. Sweeter pimentón dulce is similar to sweet paprika from Hungary and is probably the most widely used. You may also come across agridulce, which is sour, sweet and mildly spicy. If you like your food hot, look out for picante, similar to cayenne pepper. A little goes a long way.

Raisins

There are vineyards all over Spain, and as well as wine, these produce raisins that can be used for cooking. For something extra special, try to find Malaga raisins from the south of the country, which are large and have a very rich, sweet flavour to them. They are great for a simple pudding served with some cheese or a sherry.

Rice

Spain is well known for its rice, especially the Valencia region. The rice produced is mainly short to medium grain and is similar to a risotto rice. This kind of rice is excellent at retaining moisture without becoming sticky. Look out for paella rice or bomba rice for cooking Spanish dishes.

Salt cod

This preserved fish first became popular with the Basque people who have for years fished cod in the Atlantic. Search out thick pieces of cod, without too many bones. To prepare the fish, you need to start well in advance, soaking for a day, or even two, in cold water and changing the water at least twice to get rid of the excess salt. The finished product has a distinctive taste and can be used classically in fried croquettes or even to finish off a simple salad.

Saffron

The most expensive spice in the world, saffron comes from the stems of a particular crocus flower. About 200 hand-picked flowers need to be roasted to yield just 1 gram of the spice. But the distinctive yellow colour and special aroma make the expense worthwhile. You can find powdered saffron, but it's best to buy the variety that looks like little threads. These need to be soaked in a hot liquid to bring out the flavour and colour. While expensive, a little really will go a long way. For any dish you just need a pinch – maybe 15–20 threads – otherwise it will overwhelm the food and end up tasting slightly medicinal.

Sausages

The famous Spanish sausage, chorizo, is now enjoyed by people all over the world. What started out as a pale, garlicky sausage was given its distinctive colour and taste when the conquistadors introduced pepper from the New World. You'll find it in many shapes and sizes and with varying levels of heat. Most popular is soft, semi-cured chorizo, which needs to be cooked before eating (try cooking it in a little red wine or sherry), and cured chorizo, which can be sliced and eaten straight away. Less common, but also delicious, is morcilla, a blood sausage that is sometimes made with the addition of cooked rice. Black pudding can be used instead, but the sausage must always be cooked before eating.

Sherry

Sherry is a fortified wine, aged in a barrel and traditionally produced in the south of Spain around the town of Jerez. There are many types to try, ranging from dry to sweet and even creamy varieties. A Fino style is a good choice if you want a dry sherry, while an Oloroso is a delicious sweeter variety. For something a bit different, try a Manzanilla sherry, a light, dry variety with a taste of the sea, or Pedro Ximenez, which is a sweet sherry with a very rich 'raisiny' taste.

Vinegar

Like many wine countries, Spain produces a variety of red and white wine vinegars that are great for dressing a salad or adding flavour to a dish. Sherry vinegar, especially any produced in the Jerez region, is delicious and well worth trying. This kind of vinegar has a rich, dark caramel colour and a hint of sweetness to it. It's perfect to cut through the richness of pork when finishing a dish or adding to a gazpacho.

recommended equipment

Cazuelas

These attractive earthenware dishes are typically Spanish and look rustic on the outside with a glaze inside the dish. They can be used to cook over the direct flame of a gas burner or in the oven and are popular, as they heat evenly and retain their heat as well. Smaller dishes are classic for serving tapas, giving an authentic feel to the table, and as they keep warm, they are perfect for serving a leisurely meal.

Griddle pan

The sun shines a lot in Spain, but for those less fortunate with their weather a griddle pan is a good standby. These heavy pans have thick ridges on them so that when you cook food they give the charred taste and look of barbecued food.

Paella pan

These large, shallow pans are perfect for making paella; they ensure the ingredients don't disappear into the rice but remain on the surface, making for a show-stopping presentation. For cooking at home, paella pans come with a range of surfaces – nonstick, enamelled steel and stainless steel are all common. Just make sure you choose your size carefully, or prepare to cook over two or more burners, as paella pans are made to feed a large crowd.

nibbles

boquerones

Serves **6**
Preparation time **15 minutes**,
  plus marinating overnight

400 g (13 oz) **fresh
  anchovies**, gutted
100 ml (3½ fl oz) **white wine
  vinegar**
100 ml (3½ fl oz) **olive oil**
3 **garlic cloves**, sliced
½ **red chilli**, chopped
salt
1 tablespoon finely chopped
  parsley, to garnish

Open up each anchovy and pull the spine and all the bones away. Remove the heads. Rinse the fish under cold running water and pat dry with kitchen paper.

Place the anchovies in a non-metallic dish, pour over the vinegar and add a pinch of salt. Cover and leave to marinate in the refrigerator for at least 2 hours until the fish is no longer translucent. Rinse again and pat dry.

Mix together the oil, garlic and chilli in a dish, then add the anchovies, cover and marinate in the refrigerator overnight. Serve with a little of the oil and the parsley scattered over.

For boquerone salad, prepare the anchovies as above. Whisk together 2 tablespoons sherry vinegar and 6 tablespoons olive oil in a salad bowl. Add 4 baby gem lettuces, separated into leaves, 2 chopped tomatoes and 300 g (10 oz) drained boquerones and toss together. Arrange on a serving plate, scatter over 2 chopped hard-boiled eggs and serve.

roasted almonds with paprika

Serves **6**
Preparation time **5 minutes**
Cooking time **17 minutes**

300 g (10 oz) **blanched almonds**
2 teaspoons **olive oil**
1 teaspoon **sweet smoked paprika**
1 ½ teaspoons **sea salt flakes**

Place the almonds on a baking sheet and roast in a preheated oven, 180°C (350°F), Gas Mark 4, for 15 minutes until starting to brown.

Stir through the remaining ingredients, return to the oven and cook for a further 2 minutes until heated through. Leave to cool, then serve.

For roasted almond & paprika dressing, cook the almonds as above. Leave to cool, then finely chop one-third of the nuts. Place in a bowl and mix together with 2 chopped tomatoes, 2 tablespoons olive oil and a pinch of ground cumin. Serve drizzled over griddled lamb chops or chicken.

citrus olives

Serves **6**
Preparation time **5 minutes**,
  plus marinating overnight
  (optional)
Cooking time **1 minute**

2 teaspoons **fennel seeds**
finely grated rind and juice of
  ½ **lemon**
finely grated rind and juice of
  ¼ **orange**
75 ml (3 fl oz) **olive oil**
400 g (13 oz) **mixed olives**

Place the fennel seeds in a small, dry frying pan and toast for 30 seconds until they start to pop and emit an aroma. Remove from the pan and roughly crush.

Mix together the fennel seeds, lemon and orange rind and juice and oil in a non-metallic bowl, then stir in the olives. Serve immediately or cover and leave to marinate overnight in a cool place before serving.

For citrus olive butter, mix together 75 g (3 oz) finely chopped pitted olives, 50 g (2 oz) softened butter and 1 teaspoon each of grated lemon and orange rind in a bowl, then add 1 tablespoon finely chopped parsley. Spoon on to a sheet of clingfilm. Form into a tube and tightly roll up, twisting the ends to secure, then store in the freezer or refrigerator. Cut off slices to serve on top of baked or grilled white fish.

picos breadsticks

Makes **32**
Preparation time **30 minutes**,
  plus rising
Cooking time **10–15 minutes**

500 g (1 lb) **strong white
  bread flour**
2 teaspoons **fast-action
  dried yeast**
2 teaspoons **salt**
4 tablespoons **extra virgin
  olive oil**
325 ml (11 fl oz) **warm water**
1 **egg yolk**
sesame seeds, for sprinkling

Place the flour in a large bowl, add the yeast and salt, then stir in the oil and enough of the measurement water to form a firm, sticky dough. Knead the dough for about 5–10 minutes using a dough hook in an electric mixer or on a well-floured surface by hand until smooth and elastic. Put the dough in a lightly oiled bowl, cover with a tea towel and leave to rise in a warm, draught-free place for 1 hour until doubled in size.

Knock back the dough, then divide into 2 pieces and roll out each piece into a long, thick rope. Cut each rope into 16 pieces and then roll into balls. Cover loosely with a lightly oiled piece of clingfilm and leave to rest for 5 minutes.

Roll each ball into a short log and taper the ends, then place on 2 lightly greased large baking sheets, leaving a little space between them. Beat together the egg yolk and 1 tablespoon water, then brush a little over the breadsticks and sprinkle over the sesame seeds. Bake in a preheated oven, 200°C (400°F), Gas Mark 6, for 10–15 minutes until golden. Transfer to a wire rack and leave to cool.

For crispy breadstick knots, make the dough as above, then divide into 2 pieces. Shape each piece into a rectangle about 20 x 15 cm (8 x 6 inches), then cut into 16 equal-sized strips. Roll out each strip to form a long log and then tie the ends together as you would a piece of string. Place on baking sheets, brush over the egg wash and sprinkle with sesame seeds. Bake as above for 15–20 minutes until golden, then turn off the oven and leave to cool inside.

garlicky mushrooms on toast

Serves **4**
Preparation time **5 minutes**
Cooking time **5 minutes**

25 g (1 oz) **butter**
250 g (8 oz) **mixed mushrooms**,
  trimmed and halved
1 **garlic clove**, sliced
1 tablespoon **Fino sherry**
1 tablespoon **olive oil**
4 slices of **country-style bread**
salt and **pepper**

To serve
handful of chopped **parsley**
Manchego cheese shavings

Heat the butter in a frying pan, add the mushrooms and cook for 2 minutes. Add the garlic and cook for a further 1 minute until the mushrooms are lightly golden. Stir in the sherry and cook until evaporated, then season.

Meanwhile, drizzle the oil over the bread and toast in a preheated griddle pan for 1–2 minutes on each side until golden and crisp.

Spoon the mushrooms over the toast, then scatter with the parsley and Manchego cheese shavings to serve.

For baked garlic mushrooms, mash together 25 g (1 oz) softened butter, 1 crushed garlic clove and a handful of chopped parsley in a bowl. Place a little on top of 4 field mushrooms, then scatter over 25 g (1 oz) each of dried white breadcrumbs and grated Manchego cheese. Place on a lightly oiled baking sheet and bake in a preheated oven, 200°C (400°F), Gas Mark 6, for 10 minutes or until the cheese has melted and the mushrooms are cooked through.

membrillo with manchego

Serves **4–6**
Preparation time **5 minutes**,
  plus cooling
Cooking time **1¼ hours**

1.5 kg (3 lb) **quinces**, rinsed
granulated sugar (see
  method)
300 g (10 oz) **Manchego
  cheese**

Chop the quinces roughly and place in a large saucepan. Cover with water and bring to the boil, then reduce the heat and simmer for 30 minutes until soft.

Push the mixture through a sieve, then weigh the purée (it should make about 1 kg/2 lb). Return the purée to the pan with an equal amount of granulated sugar. Stir until dissolved, then simmer for about 40 minutes or until thickened and a clean line appears when you scrape through the mixture at the bottom of the pan with a spoon.

Pour into lightly oiled sterilized containers and store in the refrigerator until just set. Store for up to 6 weeks.

Cut the cheese into thick triangular slices to serve. Spoon the membrillo on top of the cheese and arrange on serving plates.

garlic & tomato toasts

Serves **4**
Preparation time **5 minutes**
Cooking time **3 minutes**

4 slices of **crusty country-style bread**
1 **fat garlic clove**, halved
2 **ripe tomatoes**, halved
2 tablespoons **extra virgin olive oil**
pinch of **sea salt flakes**
capers, **olives** or slices of **Serrano ham** to serve (optional)

Toast the bread under a preheated grill or in a griddle pan until just starting to crisp and turn golden. Rub all over 1 side of each with the cut faces of the garlic.

Rub the tomatoes over the toast, using the cut faces and making sure the tomato juices soak into the bread. Drizzle with the oil, then sprinkle over the salt flakes.

Top with capers, olives or slices of Serrano ham before serving, if liked.

For chunky tomato salsa toasts, whisk together 1 tablespoon sherry vinegar, 3 tablespoons extra virgin olive oil, a pinch of salt and 1 small crushed garlic clove in a bowl. Add 4 chopped tomatoes, 1 sliced spring onion and 1 tablespoon chopped cucumber and toss together. Toast the bread as above and spoon over the salsa to serve.

salt cod dip

Serves **6**
Preparation time **15 minutes**,
  plus soaking and standing
Cooking time **15 minutes**

300 g (10 oz) piece of **salt
  cod**
4 litres (7 pints) **cold water**
250 g (8 oz) **floury potatoes**,
  peeled and quartered
3 **garlic cloves**, crushed
125 ml (4 fl oz) **olive oil**
salt (optional)
slices of **toast**, to serve

Place the salt cod in a large dish and pour over
the measurement water. Cover and leave to soak in
the refrigerator for 24–48 hours, depending on its
thickness, changing the water at least twice. Drain, then
place the fish in a saucepan and cover with fresh cold
water. Heat just to boiling point, then remove the pan
from the heat and leave to stand for 15 minutes.

Meanwhile, cook the potatoes in a separate saucepan
of boiling salted water for 15 minutes until very tender,
then drain.

Drain the salt cold, discard any skin and bones, then
flake into small pieces. Place in a food processor
with the garlic and half the oil and pulse until it forms
a rough purée. Add the potatoes and remaining oil,
then pulse again until the mixture forms a fluffy purée.
Season with a little salt, if needed.

Spoon the dip into a serving dish and serve with slices
of toast.

For salt cod-stuffed peppers, make the salt cold
mixture as above. Drain 6 large ready-roasted red
peppers from a jar. Using a spoon, stuff the peppers
with the salt cod mixture and place on a lightly greased
baking sheet. Bake in a preheated oven, 190°C (375°F),
Gas Mark 5, for 20–25 minutes until heated through.

baby green peppers in olive oil

Serves **6**
Preparation time **5 minutes**
Cooking time **3–5 minutes**

3 tablespoons **olive oil**
250 g (8 oz) **Padrón peppers**
  or **baby green peppers, or**
  mild green chillies
sea salt flakes

Heat the oil in a large frying pan, add the peppers or chillies and cook over a high heat for 3–5 minutes, turning frequently, until the skins start to brown.

Remove from the pan and drain on kitchen paper, then serve scattered with sea salt flakes.

For charred green pepper toasts, cook the peppers as above, then leave to cool. Halve the peppers and discard the seeds, membranes and stalks, then cut into chunks. Toss together with 3 chopped tomatoes and 50 g (2 oz) chopped pitted olives in a bowl. Whisk together 1 crushed garlic clove, 1 tablespoon red wine vinegar and 3 tablespoons olive oil in a small bowl. Stir into the pepper mixture along with a handful of chopped parsley. Halve 6 large slices of country-style bread, drizzle with olive oil and toast under a preheated grill until lightly browned. Spoon the pepper mixture on top of the toasts and serve.

anchovy-stuffed eggs

Serves **6**
Preparation time **15 minutes**,
  plus cooling
Cooking time **5 minutes**

12 **quails' eggs**
2 **anchovy fillets in oil**,
  drained
2 tablespoons **extra virgin
  olive oil**
½ tablespoon **lemon juice**
1 tablespoon **capers**, drained
handful of **parsley**, chopped
salt and **pepper**

Cook the quails' eggs in a saucepan of boiling water for
3 minutes, then drain and cool under cold running water.
Shell the eggs, then slice each in half and scoop out the
yolks. Set aside.

Mash together the anchovies and oil in a bowl, stir in
the lemon juice and the egg yolks and mix together until
smooth, then season.

Spoon the anchovy mixture back into the halved eggs,
then sprinkle over the capers and parsley and serve.

For egg, anchovy & tuna bites, cook 1 hen's egg in a
saucepan of boiling water for 8 minutes until just
hard-boiled. Drain and cool under cold running water,
then shell and finely chop. Mix together 100 g (3½ oz)
tuna in oil, drained, 3 tablespoons mayonnaise and
a squeeze of lemon juice in a bowl. Toast 6 slices of
baguette under a preheated grill until crisp, then spoon
over the tuna mixture. Top with 2 anchovy fillets in oil,
drained and chopped, 1 teaspoon drained capers and
the chopped egg and serve.

chorizo & tomato loaf

Makes **1 loaf**
Preparation time **15 minutes**
Cooking time **40 minutes**

200 g (7 oz) **self-raising flour**
1 teaspoon **salt**
3 **eggs**
100 ml (3½ fl oz) **milk**
100 ml (3½ fl oz) **olive oil**
125 g (4 oz) **sun-dried tomatoes**, roughly chopped
125 g (4 oz) **cooked chorizo sausage,** chopped
100 g (3½ oz) **Manchego cheese**, grated

Tip the flour and salt into a large mixing bowl and make a well in the centre. Whisk together the eggs, milk and oil in a jug until combined, then pour into the well. Stir together until smooth, then add the tomatoes, chorizo and three-quarters of the cheese and stir until well combined.

Spoon the mixture into an oiled and base-lined 20 x 10 cm (8 x 4 inch) loaf tin and smooth the top. Scatter over the remaining cheese. Place in a preheated oven, 190°C (375°F), Gas Mark 5, for 40 minutes until golden and cooked through. Turn out on to a wire rack and leave to cool slightly. Cut into slices and eat warm or cold.

For chorizo & tomato sandwiches, heat 2 teaspoons olive oil in a frying pan, add 4 sliced medium chorizo sausages and cook for 2 minutes on each side until golden. Place 6 sun-dried tomatoes, 1 crushed garlic clove and 3 tablespoons olive oil in a small food processor or blender and pulse until the mixture forms a rough purée. Add a squeeze of lemon juice, season and pulse again. Split 4 long rolls in half. Lightly toast the cut sides under a preheated grill, then add the cooked chorizo. Spoon over the sun-dried tomato purée and top with some rocket leaves. Cut into thick slices, if liked.

garlic, chorizo & egg soup

Serves **4**
Preparation time **10 minutes**
Cooking time **15–17 minutes**

2 tablespoons **olive oil**
2–3 **garlic cloves**, finely
  chopped
125 g (4 oz) **chorizo
  sausage**, diced
6 tablespoons **red wine**
1 litre (1¾ pints) **beef** or
  game stock
2 teaspoons **tomato purée**
1 teaspoon **soft brown sugar**
4 **eggs**
salt and **pepper**
chopped **parsley**, to garnish
croûtons, to serve

Heat the oil in a saucepan, add the garlic and chorizo and fry gently for 3–4 minutes. Add the wine, stock, tomato purée and sugar, season with salt and pepper and bring to the boil, then reduce the heat and simmer for 5 minutes.

Reduce the heat to a very gentle simmer, then break the eggs, one at a time, into the pan, leaving space between them. Poach for 3–4 minutes until the whites are set and the yolks are cooked to your liking.

Check the seasoning, then transfer 1 egg into the base of each of 4 bowls, ladle over the soup and garnish with a little chopped parsley. Serve scattered with croûtons.

For garlic, chorizo & potato soup, make the soup as above, adding 375 g (12 oz) peeled and diced potatoes with the garlic and chorizo. Continue as above, omitting the eggs, and simmer for 30 minutes. Serve with garlic croûtes and grated Gruyère cheese.

chorizo & manchego buns

Makes **12 buns**
Time **1½–2½ hours**,
    depending on machine, plus
    shaping, rising and baking

225 ml (7½ fl oz) **water**
3 tablespoons **olive oil**
100 g (3½ oz) **Manchego**
    cheese, grated
1 teaspoon **salt**
1 teaspoon **hot paprika**
450 g (14½ oz) **strong white**
    bread flour
2 teaspoons **caster sugar**
1¼ teaspoons **fast-action**
    dried yeast
125 g (4 oz) **chorizo**
    sausage, diced

Lift the bread pan out of the machine and fit the blade. Put all the ingredients, except the chorizo, in the pan, following the order specified in the manufacturer's instructions.

Fit the pan into the machine and close the lid. Set to the dough programme, adding the chorizo when the machine beeps.

At the end of the programme, turn the dough out on to a floured surface and divide it into 12 equal pieces. Shape each piece into a ball. Cut 12 x 15 cm (6 inch) squares of baking paper. Push a paper square down into the section of a muffin or Yorkshire pudding tray and drop a ball of dough into it. Repeat with the remainder.

Cover loosely with a clean, dry tea towel and leave in a warm, draught-free place for 30 minutes until risen.

Use a pair of kitchen scissors to snip across the top of each bun. Bake in a preheated oven, 220°C (425°F), Gas Mark 7, for 20 minutes until risen and golden. Transfer to a wire rack to cool.

For a Serrano ham & Parmesan crown, fry 100 g (3½ oz) chopped Serrano ham in 1 tablespoon olive oil until lightly browned. Make the dough as above, using 75 g (3 oz) grated Parmesan cheese instead of the Manchego and adding the ham when the machine beeps. Once the dough is shaped into balls, fit them into a greased 20 cm (8 inch) round cake tin. Leave to rise and bake as above, but increasing the cooking time to 25–30 minutes. After baking, transfer to a wire rack to cool and serve, torn into individual buns.

fish & seafood

catalan seafood pasta

Serves **4–6**
Preparation time **15 minutes**
Cooking time **20–25 minutes**

5 tablespoons **olive oil**
1 **cleaned squid**, cut into
    rings, tentacles reserved
12 small **raw unpeeled prawns**
6 **shelled** and **cleaned scallops**
4 **garlic cloves**, thinly sliced
150 ml (¼ pint) **dry white**
    wine
400 g (13 oz) can **chopped**
    tomatoes
1 teaspoon **sweet paprika**
pinch of **saffron threads**
750 ml (1¼ pints) hot **fish** or
    chicken stock
400 g (13 oz) **angel hair** or
    fideo pasta, broken into
    3 cm (1¼ inch) pieces
salt and **pepper**
chopped **parsley**, to garnish
lemon slices, to serve

Garlic mayonnaise
2 **garlic cloves**, crushed
100 g (3½ oz) **mayonnaise**

Heat 1 tablespoon of the oil in a large frying pan, add the squid rings and tentacles and cook for 1 minute on each side or until lightly golden. Remove from the pan and set aside. Add a little more oil to the pan and cook the prawns for 1–2 minutes on each side until they turn pink. Set aside. Finally, add the scallops and cook for 1 minute, adding more oil if necessary, then set aside with any pan juices.

Add the remaining oil to the pan, add the sliced garlic and fry gently for 30 seconds. Pour in the wine and cook for a couple of minutes until reduced by half. Add the tomatoes, paprika and saffron and simmer for 5 minutes.

Stir in the stock, then add the pasta, season and stir until well coated. Cook gently for 5 minutes, adding water if necessary. Top with the cooked seafood and pan juices and cook for a further 2–5 minutes until the pasta is cooked through and the seafood is piping hot.

Meanwhile, make the garlic mayonnaise by mixing together the ingredients in a bowl. Scatter the pasta with chopped parsley and serve with lemon slices and spoonfuls of the mayonnaise.

For monkfish & chorizo pasta, replace the seafood with 400 g (13 oz) monkfish fillet. Heat 1 tablespoon olive oil in a frying pan, add the monkfish and cook for 3–5 minutes until golden and just cooked through. Remove from the pan. Add 1 tablespoon olive oil to the pan and cook 100 g (3½ oz) sliced chorizo sausage for 1 minute until starting to brown. Add the garlic and continue as above, returning the monkfish to the pan to heat through for the final 2–3 minutes of cooking.

chorizo-stuffed plaice & tomatoes

Serves **4**
Preparation time **20 minutes**
Cooking time **20–25 minutes**

100 g (3½ oz) **chorizo
sausage**, roughly chopped
50 g (2 oz) **fresh white
breadcrumbs**
2 tablespoons **sun-dried
tomato paste**
5 tablespoons **olive oil**
2 large **plaice**, cut into 8 fillets,
pin-boned and skinned
8 small **ripe tomatoes** or
4 large **tomatoes**, halved
several **thyme sprigs**
splash of **white wine**
salt and **pepper**

Put the chorizo in a food processor and pulse until finely chopped. Alternatively, chop it finely with a knife. Add the breadcrumbs, tomato paste and 1 tablespoon of the oil and process until combined.

Lay the plaice fillets, skinned-side up, on the work surface. Spread each with a thin layer of the chorizo mixture and roll up, starting from the thick end.

Place the fish in a large, shallow ovenproof dish and tuck the tomatoes and thyme around the fish. Drizzle with the remaining oil and the wine and season the fish lightly with salt and pepper.

Bake in a preheated oven, 200°C (400°F), Gas Mark 6, for 20–25 minutes or until cooked through.

For herby plaice roll-ups with tapenade, spread 1 tablespoon black olive tapenade over 1 side of 4 skinned and pin-boned plaice fillets. Mix 1 tablespoon each chopped mint and parsley and the grated rind of 1 lemon and season with salt and pepper. Sprinkle over the tapenade. Roll up the fish, starting at the thick end, and secure with a cocktail stick. Place the rolls in an ovenproof dish and roast in a preheated oven, 180°C (350°F), Gas Mark 4, for 8 minutes or until cooked through.

squid, fennel & potato salad

Serves **4**
Preparation time **15 minutes**,
   plus cooling
Cooking time **30–35 minutes**

250 g (8 oz) **new potatoes**,
   scrubbed
2 **fennel bulbs**
3 tablespoons **olive oil**
500 g (1 lb) **cleaned squid**,
   cut into rings
100 g (3½ oz) **watercress**,
   separated into leaves
salt and **pepper**

Dressing
1 **shallot**, finely chopped
1 **red chilli**, deseeded and
   chopped
finely grated rind and juice of
   1 **lemon**
1 tablespoon **capers**, drained
   and chopped
1 tablespoon chopped **mint**
2 tablespoons **olive oil**

Cook the potatoes in a saucepan of lightly salted boiling water for 15–20 minutes or until just cooked through. Drain, then leave to cool.

Reserve the fronds for garnish, then cut the fennel into thin wedges, leaving the root end intact to hold the pieces together. Put the fennel in a baking tin, drizzle with 1 tablespoon of the oil, season with salt and pepper and roast in a preheated oven, 190°C (375°F), Gas Mark 5, for 15 minutes until golden.

Meanwhile, cut the potatoes in half. Heat 1 tablespoon of the oil in a frying pan and fry the potatoes until they are crisp and golden. Drain on kitchen paper and transfer to a large salad bowl.

Make the dressing by mixing all the ingredients together in a bowl.

Heat the remaining oil in a large frying pan until it is smoking, then add the squid and carefully fry for 2–3 minutes. Add the squid to the dressing. Remove the fennel from the oven, leave to cool slightly, then add to the bowl with the squid and combine gently. Stir through the watercress and serve immediately.

For chilli squid salad, mix together 5 tablespoons plain flour, 1 tablespoon chilli powder and 1 teaspoon salt. Dust 500 g (1 lb) cleaned squid pieces in the seasoned flour and deep-fry in batches in hot oil for 2–3 minutes until crisp and golden (see page 74). Serve with sliced chilli, fresh coriander and mint leaves, sliced spring onions and lime wedges.

lemon & tomato swordfish kebabs

Serves **4**
Preparation time **10 minutes**
Cooking time **8 minutes**

350 g (11½ oz) **swordfish**,
   cut into 3 cm (1¼ inch)
   chunks
1 tablespoon **olive oil**
1 **lemon**, sliced
handful of **fresh bay leaves**
12 **cherry tomatoes**
salt and **pepper**

Toss the fish in the oil to coat, then season with salt and pepper. Chop the lemon slices in half. Thread the fish chunks on to 4 metal skewers, alternating with the lemon slices, bay leaves and tomatoes.

Heat a griddle pan until smoking hot, then add the kebabs and cook over a high heat for 4 minutes on each side or until the fish is cooked through. Serve with a mixed green salad.

For swordfish steaks with orange & tomato sauce,
heat 1 tablespoon olive oil in a large frying pan, add 2 finely chopped garlic cloves and cook for 30 seconds. Stir in a 400 g (13 oz) can chopped tomatoes and 2 strips of orange rind and simmer for 5 minutes. Add 4 swordfish steaks, about 175 g (6 oz) each, cover and simmer for 12 minutes until just cooked through. Stir through a handful of pitted green or black olives and serve with some crusty bread.

For lemony swordfish with tomato sauce, place
4 swordfish steaks, about 175 g (6 oz) each, on a plate, cover with a mixture of 1 tablespoon olive oil, the finely grated rind and juice of 1 lemon and a handful of oregano, chopped, and leave to marinate. Meanwhile, heat 1 tablespoon olive oil in a frying pan, add 2 cored, deseeded and quartered red peppers, 1 teaspoon caster sugar and 1 tablespoon white wine vinegar and cook gently for 10 minutes. Add 200 g (7 oz) cherry tomatoes and cook for a further 10–15 minutes until the vegetables are very tender. Season well. Meanwhile, cook the swordfish under a preheated hot grill for 7 minutes on each side until cooked through. Serve with the peppers and tomatoes.

grilled sea bass with salsa verde

Serves **4**
Preparation time **10 minutes**
Cooking time **12 minutes**

olive oil, for rubbing
4 **sea bass fillets**, about
   150 g (5 oz) each
salt and **pepper**

Salsa verde
3 tablespoons **olive oil**
large handful of **flat leaf
   parsley**
small handful of **basil**
1 **garlic clove**, crushed
juice of ½ **lemon**
1 tablespoon **capers**, drained

Rub a little olive oil over the fish fillets and season with salt and pepper.

Heat a griddle pan until smoking hot, add the fish fillets, skin-side down, and cook for 7 minutes until the skin is crisp and golden. Turn the fish over and cook for a further 5 minutes until just cooked through.

Meanwhile, place the salsa verde ingredients in a small food processor and whizz to a rough paste.

Place the fish on serving plates and spoon over the salsa verde. Serve with boiled new potatoes and a green salad.

For spaghetti with salsa verde & tuna, prepare the salsa verde as above, then stir in 150 g (5 oz) drained canned tuna. Meanwhile, cook 500 g (1 lb) fresh spaghetti according to the packet instructions. Drain the pasta, return to the pan and toss through the tuna and salsa verde. Serve immediately.

For sea bass stuffed with salsa verde, prepare the salsa verde as above. Divide 2 sea bass, about 1.25 kg (2½ lb) each, gutted and scaled, into fillets and season. Thinly slice 1 lemon and lay half the slices down a lightly oiled baking sheet. Cover with 2 fish fillets, skin-side down. Spread the salsa verde all over the fish, then lay the other fillets on top. Cover with the remaining lemon slices. Bake in a preheated oven, 230°C (450°F), Gas Mark 8, for 15–20 minutes until just cooked through. Place on a warm serving plate and serve with boiled new potatoes and a green salad.

seared scallops with migas

Serves **4**
Preparation time **10 minutes**,
  plus soaking
Cooking time **15 minutes**

200 g (7 oz) **country-style
  bread**, cut into small cubes
100 ml (3½ fl oz) **warm water**
pinch of **sweet paprika**
5 tablespoons **olive oil**
4 **bacon rashers**
3 **garlic cloves**
12 **shelled** and **cleaned
  plump scallops**
salt
chopped **parsley**, to garnish
lemon slices, to serve

Place the bread in a bowl. Mix the measurement water with a little salt and the paprika, then pour over the bread and leave to soak for 30 minutes.

Heat 4 tablespoons of the oil in a large frying pan, add the bacon and garlic and cook until the bacon is crisp. Remove from the pan, discard the garlic and break the bacon into small pieces.

Squeeze any excess water from the bread, then cook in the pan for 10 minutes, stirring frequently, until crisp and golden. Return the bacon pieces and heat through.

Meanwhile, in a separate frying pan, heat the remaining oil. Pat the scallops dry with kitchen paper, season with salt and then fry for 2–3 minutes on each side until golden and just cooked through. Serve sprinkled with the bacon breadcrumbs and parsley, along with lemon slices.

For scallops with bacon & tomatoes, place 3 tomatoes in a heatproof bowl and pour over boiling water to cover. Leave for 1–2 minutes, then drain, cut a cross at the stem end of each tomato and peel off the skins. Chop the flesh. Heat 2 tablespoons olive oil in a small saucepan, add 1 small finely chopped shallot and cook for 5 minutes. Stir in 1 crushed garlic clove, a pinch of dried chilli flakes and the tomatoes and cook for 5 minutes until pulpy. Meanwhile, grill 2 bacon rashers until nearly crisp, cut into small pieces and stir into the sauce. Divide 12 scallops between 4 ramekins and spoon over the sauce. Scatter over 25 g (1 oz) dried white breadcrumbs, drizzle with olive oil and bake in a preheated oven, 200°C (400°F), Gas Mark 6, for 8–10 minutes until golden and the scallops are just cooked through.

mixed seafood gril

Serves **4**
Preparation time **10 minutes**,
   plus infusing
Cooking time **15–20 minutes**

300 g (10 oz) **cleaned squid**
12 **raw, unpeeled prawns**
12 **live clams**, cleaned
   (discard any that don't shut
   when tapped)
12 **live mussels**, scrubbed
   and debearded (discard any
   that don't shut when tapped)
lemon wedges, to serve

Dressing
2 **garlic cloves**, peeled and
   bruised
6 tablespoons **extra virgin
   olive oil**
2 tablespoons chopped
   parsley

Cut the squid bodies in half lengthways, reserving the tentacles, open out and pat dry with kitchen paper. Lay them on a chopping board, shiny-side down, and, using a sharp knife, lightly score a fine diamond pattern on the flesh, then cut the squid into 3 cm (1¼ inch) squares. Chill with the squid tentacles until required.

Make the dressing. Put the garlic in a small bowl, add the oil and stir in the parsley. Leave to infuse for at least 15 minutes.

When ready to serve, heat a griddle pan over a high heat until smoking hot. Lightly brush the prawns and squid with half the dressing. Add the prawns to the pan and cook for 3–4 minutes on each side or until they turn pink. Transfer to a warm serving plate.

Add the squares of squid, scored-side down, the clams and mussels to the pan and cook for 5–7 minutes or until the squid turns white and is charred and the clams and mussels have opened. Discard any that remain closed. Add the squid tentacles and cook for a further 2–3 minutes, then transfer everything to the serving plate and drizzle all the seafood with the remaining dressing. Serve immediately with lemon wedges, Avocado Dip (see below) and bread, if liked.

For tangy avocado dip, to serve as an accompaniment, halve, stone and peel 2 very ripe, large avocados, then place in a food processor or blender with 2 tablespoons each of good-quality mayonnaise and soured cream, the juice of 1 lemon, 1 teaspoon mild chilli sauce, if liked, and some salt and pepper. Blend until smooth and spoon into a small bowl to serve.

tomato stew with clams & chorizo

Serves **4**
Preparation time **15 minutes**
Cooking time **20–25 minutes**

300 g (10 oz) **chorizo
 sausage**, cut into chunks
1 teaspoon **coriander seeds**,
 crushed
1 tablespoon **fennel seeds**,
 crushed
1 **onion**, finely chopped
1 **red chilli**, deseeded and
 finely chopped
2 **garlic cloves**, crushed
50 ml (2 fl oz) **white wine**
400 g (13 oz) can **chopped
 tomatoes**
200 ml (7 fl oz) **fish stock**
500 g (1 lb) **live clams**,
 cleaned (discard any that
 don't shut when tapped)
basil leaves, to garnish

Heat a large saucepan over a high heat, add the
chorizo and fry until the natural oil has been released
and the chorizo is starting to colour. Remove from the
pan using a slotted spoon, leaving behind the excess oil,
and set aside.

Fry the coriander and fennel seeds in the chorizo oil for
1 minute, then add the onion and chilli and fry until the
onion has softened but not coloured. Add the garlic and
fry for a further 1 minute. Pour in the wine and bubble
until reduced to 1 tablespoon.

Add the tomatoes and stock, bring to the boil and
return the chorizo to the pan. Tip in the clams, cover and
cook over a medium heat until the clams have opened.
Discard any that remain closed.

Scatter the stew with a few basil leaves and serve with
crusty bread.

For spicy bean stew with pan-fried John Dory,
follow the recipe as above, omitting the clams and
chorizo and adding a drained 400 g (13 oz) can haricot
beans and a drained 400 g (13 oz) can red kidney beans.
Pan-fry the fillets of 2 John Dory in a little olive oil until
just cooked through, then serve with the bean stew.

anchovy, red pepper & egg salad

Serves **6**

Preparation time **20 minutes**, plus cooling

Cooking time **10–15 minutes**

1 tablespoon **olive oil**

3 **red peppers**

3 **eggs**

1 tablespoon **red wine vinegar**

3 tablespoons **extra virgin olive oil**

125 g (4 oz) **rocket leaves**

100 g (3½ oz) **anchovy fillets in oil**, drained

salt and **pepper**

Rub the olive oil over the red peppers, then cook under a preheated hot grill for 10–15 minutes, turning occasionally, until blackened all over.

Meanwhile, cook the eggs in a saucepan of boiling water for 8 minutes. Drain, then cool under cold running water.

Transfer the peppers to a bowl, cover with clingfilm and leave until cool enough to handle. Peel away the blackened skin and discard the seeds, membranes and stalks then tear into strips.

Shell the eggs and cut into quarters.

Whisk together the vinegar and extra virgin olive oil in a bowl and season well. Toss the rocket with 1 tablespoon of the dressing. Arrange on a serving plate with the red peppers, eggs and anchovies, and drizzle over the remaining dressing. Serve immediately.

For anchovy, egg & red pepper sandwich, cook the eggs as above, then shell and mash together with 3 tablespoons mayonnaise in a bowl. Finely chop a drained 50 g (2 oz) can anchovy fillets in oil and add to the eggs with a little salt and pepper and a squeeze of lemon juice. Spread the mixture over 1 small halved baguette. Scatter over 1 drained and finely chopped ready-roasted red pepper from a jar and top with a handful of rocket leaves. Sandwich together and cut into smaller slices, if liked.

clams with white beans

Serves **6**
Preparation time **10 minutes**
Cooking time **15 minutes**

3 tablespoons **olive oil**
1 **onion**, chopped
1 **red chilli**, chopped
3 **garlic cloves**, sliced
125 ml (4 fl oz) **dry white wine**
400 g (13 oz) can **haricot beans**, rinsed and drained
750 g (1½ lb) **live clams**, cleaned (discard any that don't shut when tapped)
salt
chopped **parsley**, to garnish

Heat the oil in a large saucepan, add the onion and cook for 7 minutes until very soft. Add the chilli and garlic and cook for a further 1 minute. Pour in the wine and cook for 2 minutes until slightly reduced, then stir in the beans and season to taste with salt.

Tip in the clams, cover and cook over a low heat for 3–5 minutes, shaking the pan occasionally, until the clams have opened. Discard any that remain closed. Serve scattered with parsley, with some crusty bread.

For home-cooked beans, to replace the canned beans, soak 250 g (8 oz) dried haricot beans overnight in plenty of cold water. Heat 2 tablespoons olive oil in a large saucepan, add 1 chopped onion, 1 peeled and finely chopped carrot and 1 finely chopped celery stick and cook for 5 minutes until softened. Add 2 chopped garlic cloves and cook for a further 30 seconds. Drain the beans, then add to the pan with 1 litre (1¾ pints) fresh cold water. Bring to the boil, skimming away any scum, then reduce the heat and simmer for 1½ hours until the beans are soft. Drain.

olive & orange seared tuna

Serves **4–6**
Preparation time **10 minutes**
Cooking time **4–6 minutes**

500 g (1 lb) thick piece of
fresh tuna
1 teaspoon **olive oil**, plus extra
to serve
salt and **pepper**

To serve
large handful of **parsley**,
chopped
2 **garlic cloves**, finely chopped
finely grated rind of 1 **orange**
50 g (2 oz) **green olives**,
pitted and chopped

Rub the tuna with the oil and season well. Heat a large griddle pan until smoking hot, then add the tuna and cook for 2–3 minutes on each side until browned but still pink in the centre. Remove from the pan and cut into small bite-sized cubes.

Meanwhile, make the dressing by mixing together all the ingredients in a bowl.

Place the tuna on a serving plate, then sprinkle over the olive dressing. Drizzle with a little extra olive oil before serving.

For olive & orange grilled sardines, open up 8 fresh sardines like a book, then press down on the belly until flattened. Pull away the spine and remove any small bones. Rinse under cold running water and pat dry with kitchen paper. Brush all over the fish with olive oil, then cook on a preheated hot griddle pan for 3–5 minutes on each side until charred and just cooked through. Meanwhile, make the dressing as above. Serve the sardines sprinkled with the dressing.

salt cod croquettes

Serves **4**

Preparation time **25 minutes**,
  plus soaking and standing

Cooking time **25 minutes**

250 g (8 oz) piece of **salt cod**

400 g (13 oz) **potatoes**,
  peeled and quartered

1 **shallot**, grated

1 **egg yolk**

1 bunch of **parsley**, chopped

plain flour, for dusting

vegetable oil, for deep-frying

salt

lemon wedges, to serve

Soak the salt cod in cold water in the refrigerator for 24–48 hours, depending on its thickness, changing the water at least twice. Drain, then place the fish in a saucepan and cover with fresh cold water. Heat just to boiling point, then remove the pan from the heat and leave to stand for 15 minutes.

Meanwhile, cook the potatoes in a separate saucepan of lightly salted boiling water for 15 minutes until tender. Drain well, then return to the pan and mash until smooth.

Drain the salt cod, discard any skin and bones, then flake into small pieces. Squeeze away any excess water from the shallot. Stir the salt cod, shallot, egg yolk and parsley into the mashed potato. Using your hands, form the mixture into about 16 small egg shapes and dust all over with flour.

Pour the oil into a large, deep saucepan or deep fat-fryer to a depth of at least 7 cm (3 inches) and heat to 180–190°C (350–375°F), or until a cube of bread browns in 30 seconds. Deep-fry the croquettes in 2 or 3 batches for about 3 minutes, until golden, then remove with a slotted spoon. Drain on kitchen paper and keep warm while you cook the remaining croquettes. Serve warm with lemon wedges for squeezing over.

For salt cod fritters, prepare the salt cod as above. Mix together 150 g (5 oz) plain flour, 1 teaspoon baking powder, a good pinch of salt, 1 beaten egg and 150 ml (5 fl oz) milk in a bowl, then stir in the flaked salt cod. Heat 1 tablespoon olive oil in a frying pan, add spoonfuls of the batter and cook for 2 minutes on each side until golden all over. Serve with lemon wedges.

octopus with garlic dressing

Serves **6–8**

Preparation time **10 minutes**,
  plus cooling and marinating

Cooking time **1½ hours**

1 **onion**, cut into wedges

1 teaspoon **whole cloves**

1 tablespoon **salt**

2 litres (3½ pints) **water**

500 g (1 lb) **cleaned octopus**,
  bought at least
  2 days before being cooked,
  and placed in the freezer
  for 48 hours to tenderize
  the meat

Marinade

6 tablespoons **extra virgin
  olive oil**

2 **garlic cloves**, crushed

4 tablespoons chopped
  parsley

1 teaspoon **white wine
  vinegar**

salt and **pepper**

Put the onion, cloves and salt in a large saucepan, then add the measurement water and bring to the boil. Using tongs, dip the octopus in and out of the water about 4 times, returning the water to the boil before re-dipping, then immerse the octopus completely in the water. (This helps to make the flesh tender.) If there are several pieces of octopus, dip them 1 at a time.

Reduce the heat and cook the octopus very gently for 1 hour, then check to see whether it is tender. Cook for a further 15–30 minutes if necessary. Leave it to cool in the liquid, then drain, cut into bite-sized pieces and place in a non-metallic bowl.

Mix together all the marinade ingredients in a small bowl, season with salt and pepper and add to the bowl with the octopus. Mix well, cover and leave to marinate in the refrigerator for several hours or overnight. Serve the octopus with bread for mopping up the juices.

For octopus with spicy chorizo, cook the octopus as above and leave to cool, then cut into bite-sized pieces. Sprinkle 2 sliced chorizo sausages with 1 teaspoon sweet paprika and fry until crispy. Remove from the pan and drain on kitchen paper to remove the excess oil. Place 2 tablespoons olive oil in a non-metallic bowl with the juice of 1 lemon and the chorizo. Season with salt and pepper. Add the octopus, mix well to coat in the oil and cover. When ready to serve, stir in 1 tablespoon chopped fresh coriander leaves and 1 tablespoon chopped parsley. Serve with bread.

spanish fish stew

Serves **4**
Preparation time **12 minutes**
Cooking time **25 minutes**

2 tablespoons **olive oil**
1 large **red onion**, sliced
4 **garlic cloves**, chopped
1 teaspoon **smoked paprika**
  or **hot smoked paprika**
pinch of **saffron threads**
350 g (11½ oz) **monkfish**
  fillet, cut into chunks
250 g (8 oz) **red mullet fillets**,
  cut into large chunks
3 tablespoons **dry** or **medium-**
  dry Madeira
250 ml (8 fl oz) **fish** or
  vegetable stock
2 tablespoons **tomato purée**
400 g (13 oz) can **chopped**
  tomatoes
2 **bay leaves**
750 g (1½ lb) **live mussels**,
  scrubbed and debearded
  (discard any that don't
  shut when tapped) or
  250 g (8 oz) **cooked**
  shelled mussels
salt and **pepper**
3 tablespoons chopped
  parsley, to garnish

Heat the oil in a large, heavy-based saucepan over a medium-low heat, add the onion and garlic and cook gently for 8–10 minutes or until softened. Stir in the paprika and saffron and cook for a further 1 minute.

Stir in the fish, then pour over the Madeira. Add the stock, tomato purée, tomatoes and bay leaves and season with salt and pepper. Bring to the boil, then reduce the heat and simmer gently for 5 minutes.

Tip in the live mussels, cover and cook over a low heat for about 5 minutes or until the mussels have opened. Discard any that remain closed. Alternatively, if using cooked shelled mussels, simmer the stew for 2–3 minutes more or until the fish is cooked and tender, then stir in the cooked mussels. Cook for 30 seconds or until the mussels are heated through and piping hot.

Scatter with the parsley and serve immediately with crusty bread.

For pan-fried red mullet with tomato sauce, cook the onion and garlic and then the spices as above. Pour in the Madeira, add the tomatoes with the finely grated zest of ½ lemon, a pinch of sugar and season with salt and pepper. Simmer for 15–20 minutes. Heat 1–2 tablespoons olive oil in a nonstick skillet, add 500 g (1 lb) red mullet fillets, skin-side down, and fry for 2–3 minutes or until crisp. Cover, reduce the heat and cook for a further 2 minutes or until the fish is just cooked through. Serve with the tomato sauce.

squid with lemon mayonnaise

Serves **4**
Preparation time **30 minutes**
Cooking time **10 minutes**

500 g (1 lb) **cleaned squid**
50 g (2 oz) **plain flour**
1 tablespoon **sweet paprika**
pinch of **cayenne pepper**
olive oil, for deep-frying
salt and **pepper**
lemon wedges, to serve

Lemon mayonnaise
2 **egg yolks**
½ teaspoon **wholegrain
   mustard**
1 tablespoon **lemon juice**,
   plus extra to taste
200 ml (7 fl oz) **light olive oil**
1 tablespoon chopped **flat
   leaf parsley**, plus extra
   to garnish
1 tablespoon chopped **chervil**
1 tablespoon chopped **chives**
2 tablespoons chopped
   watercress
finely grated rind of **1 lemon**
1 small **garlic clove**, crushed

Make the mayonnaise. Beat the egg yolks in a bowl
with the mustard and lemon juice. Gradually add
the oil, a drop at a time, whisking constantly until it
is incorporated and forms a thick, smooth emulsion.
Season and stir in the herbs, watercress, lemon rind and
garlic, adding extra lemon juice to taste. Cover and chill
until required.

Pat the squid dry with kitchen paper and cut the bodies
into rings about 2 cm (¾ inch) thick, reserving the
tentacles. Mix together the flour, paprika and cayenne
and season well. Put the flour in a plastic bag, add the
squid rings and tentacles and shake until coated.

Pour the oil into a large, deep saucepan or deep-fat
fryer to a depth of at least 7 cm (3 inches) and heat
to 180–190°C (350-375°F), or until a cube of bread
browns in 30 seconds. Remove about one-third of the
squid from the bag and shake off the excess flour.
Carefully drop the squid into the oil and deep-fry in
batches for 2–3 minutes until crisp and golden, then
remove with a slotted spoon. Drain on kitchen paper
and keep warm while you cook the remaining squid.

Transfer the squid to serving plates, scatter with parsley
and salt and serve with lemon wedges and the mayonnaise.

For stir-fried squid, prepare and season the squid as
above. Stir-fry in 6 tablespoons olive oil. Remove, drain
and keep warm while you cook 1 sliced onion, 1 sliced
green pepper, 2 crushed garlic cloves, 1 bay leaf, 450 g
(14½ oz) chopped tomatoes and 50 g (2 oz) pitted
black olives until tender. Return the squid to the pan,
sprinkle over 4 tablespoons chopped parsley and serve.

mussels in saffron broth

Serves **6**
Preparation time **10 minutes**
Cooking time **10 minutes**

1 tablespoon **olive oil**
2 **garlic cloves**, sliced
pinch of **saffron threads**
125 ml (4 fl oz) **dry white
wine**
1 kg (2 lb) **live mussels**,
scrubbed and debearded
(discard any that don't shut
when tapped)
125 g (4 oz) **cherry tomatoes**,
halved
chopped **parsley**, to garnish

Heat the oil in a large saucepan, add the garlic and cook for 30 seconds until starting to sizzle. Add the saffron and wine and bring to the boil, then simmer for a couple of minutes.

Tip in the mussels and tomatoes, cover and cook for about 5 minutes or until the mussels have opened. Discard any that remain closed. Scatter with chopped parsley and serve with plenty of crusty bread.

For mussel & prawn stew, prepare 500 g (1 lb) live mussels as above. Heat 2 tablespoons olive oil in a large saucepan, add 1 finely chopped onion and cook for 5 minutes until softened. Stir in 2 chopped garlic cloves and cook for a further 30 seconds. Pour in 75 ml (3 fl oz) dry white wine and a pinch of saffron threads and cook until reduced by half. Add a 400 g (13 oz) can chopped tomatoes and simmer for 10 minutes, adding a little water if necessary. Tip in the cleaned mussels, cover and simmer for 4 minutes. Add 250 g (8 oz) cooked peeled prawns and cook for a further 1–2 minutes until the prawns are heated through and the mussels have opened. Discard any that remain closed. Serve scattered with chopped parsley.

seared chilli & garlic prawns

Serves **4**
Preparation time **5 minutes**
Cooking time **5 minutes**

5 tablespoons **olive oil**
3 **garlic cloves**, chopped
pinch of **dried chilli flakes**
500 g (1 lb) large **raw peeled
prawns**
handful of **parsley**, chopped
salt and **pepper**

Heat the oil in a large frying pan, add the garlic and cook for 30 seconds, then add the chilli flakes and prawns and cook for a further 2 minutes until golden.

Sprinkle over the parsley and turn the prawns over. Cook for a further 1–2 minutes until the prawns turn pink and are just cooked through. Season with salt and pepper and serve immediately.

For prawns with mushrooms & sherry, heat the oil as above, add 200 g (7 oz) trimmed oyster mushrooms and cook for 2–3 minutes until softened and golden. Stir in the chopped garlic as above and cook for 30 seconds. Pour in 100 ml (3½ fl oz) Fino sherry and cook for a couple of minutes until the liquid has reduced. Add 500 g (1 lb) large cooked peeled prawns and heat through until piping hot. Serve immediately scattered with chopped parsley.

grilled sardines with tomato salsa

Serves **1**
Preparation time **10 minutes**
Cooking time **3–4 minutes**

3 **fresh sardines**, about 125 g
   (4 oz) in total, gutted
4 tablespoons **lemon juice**
1 tablespoon chopped **basil**
salt and **pepper**

Tomato salsa
8 **cherry tomatoes**, chopped
1 **spring onion**, sliced
1 tablespoon chopped **basil**
½ **red pepper**, cored,
   deseeded and chopped

Make the tomato salsa by mixing together all the ingredients in a bowl.

Place the sardines on a baking sheet and drizzle with the lemon juice. Season with salt and pepper. Cook the sardines under a preheated hot grill for 3–4 minutes or until cooked through, turning once.

Sprinkle with the chopped basil and serve immediately with the tomato salsa and toasted ciabatta.

For quick sardine & anchovy toasts, cook the sardines as above, then place in a food processor or blender with a drained 50 g (2 oz) can anchovy fillets in oil, 1 crushed garlic clove, 1 parsley sprig and 2 tablespoons olive oil. Whizz to a paste, then spread over slices of toasted ciabatta, sprinkle with chopped parsley and serve.

caramelized onion & anchovy tart

Serves **4**
Preparation time **25 minutes**,
  plus chilling
Cooking time **55 minutes–**
  1 hour

25 g (1 oz) **butter**
2 tablespoons **olive oil**
3 **large onions**, finely sliced
2 **thyme sprigs**
2 **eggs**
100 ml (3½ fl oz) **milk**
100 ml (3½ fl oz) **double**
  cream
2 **tomatoes**, thinly sliced
8 canned **anchovy fillets in**
  oil, drained
salt and **pepper**

Pastry
200 g (7 oz) **plain flour**
85 g (3¼ oz) cold **lightly**
  salted butter, cubed
1 **egg**
1 **egg yolk**

Make the pastry. Place all the pastry ingredients in a food processor and blend until they form a soft dough, adding a drop of cold water if necessary. Knead lightly until smooth, then wrap in clingfilm and chill for at least 30 minutes.

Roll out the pastry on a lightly floured work surface until about 3 mm (⅛ inch) thick and use to line a 23 cm (9 inch) fluted tart tin. Trim off the excess pastry and chill for 1 hour.

Line the tart with baking paper and fill with baking beans. Bake in a preheated oven, 180°C (350°F), Gas Mark 4, for 10–12 minutes until lightly golden. Remove the baking paper and beans, then return to the oven and cook for a further 2 minutes to dry out the base. Remove from the oven and leave to cool, leaving the oven on.

Meanwhile, heat the butter and oil in a frying pan, add the onions and thyme and fry over a low heat for about 20 minutes until the onions are golden brown.

Remove the thyme and spread the onions over the tart base. Whisk together the eggs, milk and cream in a bowl, season with salt and pepper and pour over the onions.

Bake in the oven for 10 minutes until slightly risen and starting to set. Arrange the tomatoes and anchovies on top of the tart, then return to the oven and cook for a further 10–15 minutes until the filling has set completely. Leave to cool for 5 minutes before serving.

mixed seafood salad

Serves **6**

Preparation **20 minutes**, plus cooling

Cooking time **10 minutes**

125 ml (4 fl oz) **dry white wine**

200 g (7 oz) **live mussels**, scrubbed and debearded (discard any that don't shut when tapped)

8 large **raw prawns**, peeled with tails left on

1 **cleaned squid**, cut into rings

75 g (3 oz) **cherry tomatoes**, halved

¼ small **cucumber**, chopped

1 **green pepper**, cored, deseeded and chopped

1 tablespoon finely chopped **red onion**

large handful of **parsley**, chopped

Dressing

1 **garlic clove**, crushed

1 tablespoon **red wine vinegar**

3 tablespoons **extra virgin olive oil**

salt and **pepper**

Heat the wine in a large saucepan until simmering, then tip in the mussels, cover and cook for about 5 minutes until the mussels have opened. Remove from the pan, discard any that remain closed and leave to cool. When the mussels are cool, remove the meat from half the shells.

Meanwhile, add the prawns to the pan and cook for 3 minutes or until they turn pink and are just cooked through, then leave to cool.

Add the squid rings and tentacles to the pan and cook for 1–2 minutes until they turn white. Remove with a slotted spoon, reserving the cooking liquid, and leave to cool.

Make the dressing. Place the garlic in a small bowl and season. Add the vinegar, then whisk in the oil. Add a little of the cooled cooking liquid. Toss 2 tablespoons of the dressing together with the cooled prawns, squid, mussel meat and the mussels in their shells, then toss in the tomatoes, cucumber and green pepper. Arrange on a serving plate, scatter over the onion and parsley and drizzle with more dressing to serve.

For mixed seafood with tomato & red pepper dressing, cook and cool the seafood as above, then arrange on a serving plate. Make the dressing as above, adding an extra 2 tablespoons extra virgin olive oil and some more cooking liquid if needed. Stir in 1 finely chopped tomato, ½ drained and roughly chopped ready-roasted red pepper from a jar, 2 tablespoons drained capers and a good handful of chopped parsley. Drizzle over the salad to serve.

crispy whitebait & chip cones

Makes **12 cones**
Preparation time **20 minutes**
Cooking time **10 minutes**

250 g (8 oz) **potatoes**, peeled
    and cut into long, thin chips
sunflower oil, for deep-frying
4 tablespoons **plain flour**
400 g (13 oz) **whitebait**
salt and **pepper**
mayonnaise, to serve

Line a large sheet of newspaper with greaseproof paper, cut the double layer into 12 squares and twist each into a small cone.

Rinse the potatoes under cold running water and dry thoroughly on kitchen paper.

Pour the oil into a large, deep saucepan or deep-fat fryer to a depth of at least 7 cm (3 inches) and heat to 180–190°C (350–375°F), or until a cube of bread browns in 30 seconds. Deep-fry the chips for 4–5 minutes, then drain on kitchen paper. Deep-fry them again for 1–2 minutes until crisp and golden. Drain and keep warm.

Place the flour on a large plate and season well with salt and pepper. Toss the whitebait in the flour and fry in batches for 1–2 minutes or until crisp and golden. Drain on kitchen paper.

Toss the whitebait with the chips, season with salt and pile into the paper cones. Serve with mayonnaise.

For whitebait with Moorish spiced sweet potato wedges, peel 2 large sweet potatoes and cut into wedges. Place in a bowl with 2 tablespoons vegetable oil and 1 teaspoon each of ground cumin, ground coriander and lightly crushed fennel seeds and toss together until well combined. Spread on a nonstick baking sheet and roast in a preheated oven, 200°C (400°F), Gas Mark 6, for 30 minutes until tender in the centre and crispy on the outside. Meanwhile, cook the whitebait as above, then serve tossed with the potato wedges.

prawn & spinach scrambled eggs

Serves **4**
Preparation time **10 minutes**
Cooking time **8–10 minutes**

1 tablespoon **olive oil**
150 g (5 oz) **small raw
  peeled prawns**
75 g (3 oz) **spinach leaves**
4 **eggs**
1 **egg yolk**
25 g (1 oz) **butter**, cubed
pinch of **hot smoked paprika**,
  for sprinkling
salt and **pepper**

Heat the oil in a frying pan, add the prawns and cook for 3 minutes, turning once, until they turn pink and are cooked through. Remove from the pan and set aside.

Place the spinach in a large colander and pour over boiling water until wilted. Leave to cool slightly, then squeeze out any excess water.

Break the eggs into the pan and add the egg yolk, then season and scatter over the butter. Cook over a low heat for a couple of minutes until the whites begin to set.

Stir in the spinach and prawns, gently breaking up the yolks. Cook for a further 1–2 minutes until the egg is just set and the prawns are piping hot. Serve sprinkled with a little paprika.

For prawn, spinach & ham baked eggs, prepare the spinach as above, then finely chop and divide between 4 greased ramekins. Top with 4 chopped slices of Serrano ham and 75 g (3 oz) small cooked peeled prawns. Break 1 egg into each ramekin, place a slice of butter on top and sprinkle with a little smoked paprika. Arrange the ramekins on baking sheet and bake in a preheated oven, 200°C (400°F), Gas Mark 6, for 10–15 minutes until the eggs are just set.

scallops with citrus dressing

Serves **4**
Preparation time **10 minutes**
Cooking time **7–9 minutes**

16 large **raw peeled prawns**
   with tails left on
24 shelled and cleaned
   scallops, corals removed
1 large ripe but firm **mango**,
   peeled, stoned and cut into
   chunks
1 tablespoon **olive oil**
125 g (4 oz) **mixed salad**
   leaves

Citrus dressing
juice of ½ **pink grapefruit**
finely grated rind and juice of
   1 lime
1 teaspoon **clear honey**
1 tablespoon **raspberry**
   vinegar
75 ml (3 fl oz) **lemon oil**

Make the citrus dressing by mixing together all the ingredients in a small bowl.

Poach the prawns in a saucepan of simmering water for 2 minutes, then drain.

Put the scallops, mango and prawns in a bowl and pour over 3 tablespoons of the dressing. Mix well to coat before threading them alternately on to 8 skewers.

Heat the oil in a large frying pan over a medium heat, add the skewers and fry for about 5–7 minutes, turning and basting occasionally, until golden brown and cooked through.

Arrange the skewers on serving plates with the salad leaves and serve with the remaining dressing.

For haloumi & mango kebabs with citrus dressing, replace the scallops and prawns with 450–500 g (14½ oz–1 lb) haloumi cheese, cut into cubes. Coat with the dressing, skewer with the mango and fry as above. Alternatively, cook on a barbecue for the same amount of time until slightly charred.

crispy salt cod & chorizo salad

Serves **4**

Preparation time **15 minutes**, plus soaking

Cooking time **20 minutes**

500 g (1 lb) piece of **salt cod**
5 litres (8¾ pints) **cold water**
225 g (7½ oz) **chorizo sausage**, sliced
1 **red pepper**, cored, deseeded and finely sliced
3 large handfuls of **mixed salad leaves**
3 **spring onions**, finely sliced
200 g (7 oz) **frozen peas**, thawed
1 **celery stick**, finely sliced

Dressing

1 tablespoon **wholegrain mustard**
1 teaspoon **clear honey**
4 tablespoons **olive oil**
1 tablespoon **lemon juice**
salt and **pepper**

Place the salt cod in a large dish and pour over the measurement water. Cover and leave to soak in the refrigerator for 24–48 hours, depending on its thickness, changing the water at least twice. Drain, then place the fish in a saucepan and cover with fresh cold water. Bring to the boil, then reduce the heat and simmer for 5 minutes. Remove the fish and, when cool enough to handle, discard any skin and bones, then flake into large chunks. Set aside.

Heat a large frying pan over a medium heat, add the chorizo and cook for 2 minutes until brown. Turn the slices over, add the salt cod and cook until the chorizo and cod are crispy. Remove from the pan with a slotted spoon, leaving behind the excess oil from the chorizo. Fry the red pepper in the chorizo oil for 2 minutes. Remove from the pan.

Mix together the salad leaves, spring onions, peas and celery in a bowl. Whisk together the dressing ingredients. Add enough of the dressing to coat the salad leaves. Place the dressed salad on a serving plate and top with the crispy chorizo, salt cod and red pepper.

For salt cod salad with chickpeas, rocket & tomato, soak the fish as above, then cut into 5 cm (2 inch) chunks. Heat 1 tablespoon olive oil in a frying pan, add 300 g (10 oz) halved cherry tomatoes and 1 crushed garlic clove and cook until softened and starting to break down. Add a rinsed and drained 400 g (13 oz) can chickpeas and 2 handfuls of rocket leaves. Season with salt and pepper. Heat a little more olive oil in a separate frying pan and fry the cod until crispy. Stir through the tomatoes and chickpeas. Serve with crusty bread.

spicy grilled crab

Serves **4**
Preparation **25 minutes**
Cooking time **20 minutes**

4 small **cooked crabs**
5 tablespoons **olive oil**
1 **shallot**, finely chopped
1 small **leek**, trimmed, cleaned
   and finely chopped
1 **garlic clove**, crushed
pinch of **dried chilli flakes**
4 **tomatoes**, chopped
25 g (1 oz) **dried white
   breadcrumbs**
handful of **parsley**, chopped
salt and **pepper**

Twist off the crab claws and set aside. Lay each crab on its back and use your fingers to push away the legs and centre of the crab, then pull away the soft gills at the centre of the crab and discard. Use a heavy knife to cut the inside into 4 pieces and using a skewer, remove the flesh. Scoop out the brown meat from the centre, then use a rolling pin to tap open the legs and claws and remove the white meat.

Heat 4 tablespoons of the oil in a frying pan, add the shallot and leek and cook over a low heat for 10 minutes until softened and golden. Add the garlic and cook, stirring, for 30 seconds. Stir in the chilli flakes, tomatoes and any crab liquid and cook for a further 5 minutes until pulpy. Stir through the crabmeat and season well.

Spoon the mixture into 4 gratin dishes. Mix together the breadcrumbs, parsley and the remaining oil in a bowl, then scatter over the crabmeat. Cook under a preheated medium grill for 3–5 minutes until crisp and golden.

For spicy crab tarts, roll out 250 g (8 oz) ready-made shortcrust pastry on a lightly floured work surface until 3 mm (⅛ in) thick. Using a bowl as a template, cut out 4 circles and use to line 4 individual tart tins 8 cm (3 in) in diameter. Trim off the excess pastry. Line the tarts with baking paper and fill with baking beans. Bake in a preheated oven, 200°C (400°F), Gas Mark 6, for 7 minutes. Remove the paper and beans, then cook for a further 3–5 minutes until crisp and golden. Remove from the oven and leave to cool, leaving the oven on. Prepare the crab filling as above, then use to fill the cooled pastry cases and sprinkle with the breadcrumbs as above. Bake in the oven for 5–7 minutes until heated through and the breadcrumbs are crisp.

crisp fried seafood

Serves **4–6**
Preparation time **20 minutes**
Cooking time **5 minutes**

500 g (1 lb) **mixed seafood,**
  such as **whitebait, skinned**
  white fish fillets and
  cleaned **squid**
1 **spring onion,** finely chopped
1 **mild red chilli,** deseeded
  and thinly sliced
1 **garlic clove,** finely chopped
2 tablespoons chopped
  parsley
100 g (3½ oz) **semolina flour**
½ teaspoon **sweet paprika**
sunflower oil, for deep-frying
salt and **pepper**
lemon or **lime wedges,**
  to serve

Cut the white fish into small chunks. Slice the squid bodies into rings and pat dry on kitchen paper with the tentacles and any other seafood you might be using.

Mix together the spring onion, chilli, garlic, parsley and some salt in a bowl. Set aside.

Place the semolina flour and paprika on a plate and season lightly with salt and pepper. Add the seafood and coat well.

Pour the oil into a large, deep saucepan or deep-fat fryer to a depth of at least 7 cm (3 inches) and heat to 180–190°C (350–375°F), or until a cube of bread browns in 30 seconds. Deep-fry the fish in batches for 30–60 seconds until crisp and golden, then remove with a slotted spoon. Drain on kitchen paper and keep warm while you cook the remaining seafood. Serve in little dishes, sprinkled with the spring onion and herb mixture along with lemon or lime wedges, or Sweet Chilli Mayonnaise (see below).

For sweet chilli mayonnaise, to serve as an accompaniment, mix together 4 tablespoons mayonnaise and 1 tablespoon sweet chilli sauce in a bowl. Squeeze the juice of ½ lemon into the mayonnaise and mix well. Add a little chopped chilli if you like it hot.

langoustines with saffron aioli

Serves **8**
Preparation time **10 minutes**,
   plus infusing

pinch of **saffron threads**
2 teaspoons **boiling water**
2 **garlic cloves**, crushed
1 **egg yolk**
125 ml (4 fl oz) **extra virgin
   olive oil**
125 ml (4 fl oz) **sunflower oil**
squeeze of **lemon juice**,
   to taste
24 **cooked langoustines**
salt

Put the saffron in a small heatproof bowl and pour over
the measurement water. Leave for 10 minutes to infuse.

Mix together the garlic and egg yolk in a bowl.
Gradually whisk in the oils, a drop at a time, increasing
the amount of oil added as it starts to thicken. When all
the oil has been added and the mixture has thickened,
stir in the saffron water and season with salt and a little
lemon juice to taste.

Serve the langoustines with the aioli for dipping.

For creamy saffron & langoustine pasta, remove
the meat from the langoustine tails and set aside, or
replace with 300 g (10 oz) cooked peeled prawns.
Infuse the saffron as above. Cook 400 g (13 oz)
spaghetti according to the packet instructions.
Meanwhile, heat 2 tablespoons olive oil in a saucepan,
add 2 sliced garlic cloves and cook for 30 seconds,
then pour in 100 ml (3½ fl oz) dry white wine and
cook for 3–5 minutes until reduced by half. Stir in 75 ml
(3 fl oz) single cream and the saffron water and cook
for a further 2 minutes. Drain the pasta, then return
to the pan. Stir in the saffron sauce, langoustines or
prawns and 1 egg yolk. Stir together until the pasta is
well coated with the sauce, adding a little of the cooking
water to loosen if necessary. Serve scattered with
chopped parsley, if liked.

squid with lemon & caper dressing

Serves **4**
Preparation time **10 minutes**,
  plus marinating
Cooking time **5 minutes**

8 small or 4 large cleaned
  squid
2 tablespoons **olive oil**
1 teaspoon **ground cumin**
grated rind and juice of
  1 **lemon**
50 ml (2 fl oz) **white wine**
2 tablespoons **capers**, drained
salt and **pepper**

Halve the squid bodies lengthways, discarding the tentacles, open out and pat dry with kitchen paper. Lay them on a chopping board, shiny-side down, and, using a sharp knife, lightly score a fine diamond pattern on the flesh, being careful not to cut all the way through. Place the squid in a non-metallic bowl with the oil, cumin, lemon rind, half the lemon juice and a little pepper (no salt at this stage). Cover and leave to marinate in the refrigerator for at least 30 minutes or preferably overnight.

Heat a frying pan until smoking hot, then add the squid in batches, scored-side down, and cook for about 1–2 minutes or until it turns white and loses its transparency. Remove from the pan and keep warm while you cook the remaining squid.

Deglaze the pan with the wine and allow it to boil for 1 minute to burn off the alcohol. Remove the pan from the heat and add the remaining lemon juice and finally the capers. Season the squid with salt and pepper, pour over the pan juices and serve with Mixed Herb Salad (see below), if liked.

For mixed herb salad, to serve as an accompaniment, mix together a large handful of parsley leaves with a small handful each of mint and fresh coriander leaves in a salad bowl. In another bowl, mix together 2 tablespoons each of lemon juice and olive oil and 1 crushed garlic clove. Pour the dressing over the herb salad.

meat

spanish meatballs

Serves **4–6**

Preparation time **20 minutes**, plus soaking

Cooking time **1 hour**

50 g (2 oz) **white bread**, crusts removed

½ **onion**, grated

375 g (12 oz) **minced pork**

125 g (4 oz) **minced veal** or **chicken**

3 **garlic cloves**, crushed

handful of **parsley**, chopped

1 **egg**

2 tablespoons **olive oil**

salt and **pepper**

Tomato sauce

2 tablespoons **olive oil**

1 **onion**, finely chopped

2 **garlic cloves**, crushed

1 teaspoon **sweet smoked paprika**

125 ml (4 fl oz) **dry white wine**

400 g (13 oz) can **chopped tomatoes**

1 **thyme sprig**

Break up the bread, place in a bowl and add enough water to cover, then leave to soak for 5 minutes. Drain, then squeeze to remove the excess water and return to the bowl.

Squeeze the grated onion to remove most of the juice and add to the bread. Stir in the meat, garlic and parsley, then add the egg, season and mix together. Shape the mixture into walnut-sized balls using wet hands.

Heat the oil in a large frying pan, add the meatballs in 2 batches and fry for 5 minutes, turning occasionally, until golden all over. Set aside.

Make the sauce. Heat the oil in a large saucepan, add the onion and cook for 5 minutes until softened. Stir in the garlic and paprika and cook for a further 30 seconds. Pour in the wine and cook for 2 minutes until reduced by half. Add the tomatoes and thyme, season and simmer for 10 minutes. Add the meatballs to the sauce and simmer for 30 minutes until the meatballs are cooked through, adding a little water if necessary.

For meatballs with almond sauce, make and fry the meatballs as above, then set aside. Place 50 g (2 oz) blanched almonds, 3 crushed garlic cloves, a pinch of saffron threads, ½ teaspoon paprika and 1 tablespoon olive oil in a small food processor and blend until smooth. Heat 2 tablespoons olive oil in a saucepan, add 1 small finely chopped onion and cook for 5 minutes until softened. Pour in 150 ml (¼ pint) dry white wine and 250 ml (8 fl oz) chicken stock and bring to the boil, then simmer for 5 minutes. Add the fried meatballs and cook for 15 minutes. Stir in the almond paste and cook for a further 5 minutes until the meatballs are cooked through.

chicken liver & sherry salad

Serves **4–6**

Preparation time **5 minutes**

Cooking time **10–15 minutes**

4 tablespoons **olive oil**

400 g (13 oz) **chicken livers**, rinsed and cut into bite-sized pieces

1 **shallot**, finely chopped

125 ml (4 fl oz) **Fino sherry**

1 teaspoon **sherry vinegar**

125 g (4 oz) **rocket leaves**

Heat 1 tablespoon of the oil in a large frying pan, add half the livers and cook for 2–3 minutes, turning once, until firm and just cooked through. Remove from the pan and set aside. Repeat with the remaining livers.

Add another 1 tablespoon of the oil to the pan, add the shallot and cook for 3–5 minutes until softened. Return the livers to the pan with the sherry and cook for a couple of minutes until the liquid has reduced.

Meanwhile, whisk together the vinegar and remaining oil in a bowl, add the rocket and toss together. Arrange the rocket on serving plates, spoon over the warm livers and sauce and serve.

For chicken livers in sherry, tip the prepared livers into a bowl and pour over 150 ml (¼ pint) Fino sherry. Cover and leave to marinate in the refrigerator for 2 hours, then drain and pat dry. Season with salt and pepper and dust with a little smoked paprika. Cook in 2 batches as above until firm. Spoon on to serving plates with the juices and serve sprinkled with chopped parsley.

106

fennel & citrus pork belly

Serves **6–8**
Preparation time **10 minutes**
Cooking time **1 hour
20 minutes**

3 **garlic cloves**, crushed
1 tablespoon **fennel seeds**
finely grated rind of 1 **lemon**
finely grated rind of ½ **orange**
1.5 kg (3 lb) **boneless pork
belly**, skin scored
salt and **pepper**

Mix together the garlic, fennel seeds and lemon and orange rind in a bowl to make a paste. Rub all over the pork, pressing it into the cuts in the skin. Season well.

Place the meat in a roasting tin. Roast in a preheated oven, 220°C (425°F), Gas Mark 7, for 20 minutes. Reduce the oven temperature to 180°C (350°F), Gas Mark 4, and cook for a further 1 hour until the meat is crisp and cooked through.

Cut the meat into small bite-sized pieces and serve.

For fennel & citrus pork bites, mix together 400 g (13 oz) minced pork, 2 chopped spring onions, 2 crushed garlic cloves, 1 egg yolk, 50 g (2 oz) fresh white breadcrumbs, 1 teaspoon fennel seeds and 1 tablespoon each of finely grated lemon and orange rind in a large bowl. Shape into walnut-sized balls. Heat 1 tablespoon olive oil in a frying pan, add half the balls and cook for 10 minutes until browned and cooked through. Remove from the pan and keep warm while you cook the remaining meatballs.

romesco chicken wings

Serves **6–8**
Preparation time **25 minutes**
Cooking time **45 minutes**

16 **chicken wings**, tip ends
  removed
1 tablespoon **olive oil**
salt and **pepper**
lemon wedges, to serve

Romesco sauce
100 g (3½ oz) **blanched
  almonds**
3 tablespoons **olive oil**
2 **ready-roasted red peppers**
  from a jar, drained and
  chopped
2 **garlic cloves**, crushed
1 tablespoon **sherry vinegar**
½ teaspoon **sweet smoked
  paprika**

Toss the chicken wings together with the oil and
season well. Place on a baking sheet and bake in a
preheated oven, 200°C (400°F), Gas Mark 6, for
45 minutes until golden and cooked through.

Meanwhile, make the romesco sauce. Place the
almonds in a dry frying pan and toast for 3–5 minutes,
shaking the pan frequently, until lightly browned. Leave
to cool slightly, then place in a food processor and pulse
until roughly chopped. Add the remaining ingredients
and blend together, then season with salt and pepper.

Place the sauce in a serving bowl and serve with
the chicken for dipping in and lemon wedges for
squeezing over.

For romesco-stuffed chicken, make the romesco
sauce as above, omitting the olive oil. Stir in 2 tablespoons
crème fraîche. Using a small, sharp knife, cut down the
sides of 4 boneless, skinless chicken breasts, about
125 g (4 oz) each, to form small pockets. Spoon in the
romesco mixture, then smooth over with your fingers
to seal. Place on a baking tray, season with salt and
pepper and drizzle over a little olive oil. Roast in a
preheated oven, 190°C (375°F), Gas Mark 5, for
15 minutes or until the chicken is cooked through.

lamb skewers with aubergine dip

Serves **6–8**
Preparation time **15 minutes**,
  plus marinating
Cooking time **25–30 minutes**

3 tablespoons **olive oil**
finely grated rind of 1 **lemon**
1 teaspoon **sweet smoked**
  paprika
handful of **thyme sprigs**,
  leaves stripped and chopped
625 g (1¼ lb) diced **leg of**
  lamb

Aubergine dip
2 **aubergines**
1 tablespoon **olive oil**
1 small **garlic clove**, crushed
3 tablespoons **natural yogurt**
squeeze of **lemon juice**
salt and **pepper**

Mix together the oil, lemon rind, paprika and thyme in a non-metallic bowl. Add the lamb and mix together until well coated. Cover and leave to marinate in the refrigerator for at least 2 hours and up to 12 hours.

When ready to serve, prick the aubergines once or twice with a fork. Cook under a preheated hot grill, turning every couple of minutes, until charred and browned all over. Leave to cool slightly, then cut in half lengthways. Scoop out the soft flesh into a blender and discard the skins. Add the oil, garlic, yogurt and lemon juice, then whizz until smooth and season.

Thread the lamb on to 12–15 metal skewers. Heat a griddle pan until smoking hot, then add the skewers and cook for 5–7 minutes on each side until browned and just cooked through. Serve with the aubergine dip.

For lamb-stuffed aubergines, halve 3 aubergines, drizzle with a little oil and place in a roasting tin, then season. Roast in a preheated oven, 200°C (400°F), Gas Mark 6, for 25–30 minutes until soft. Meanwhile, heat 2 tablespoons olive oil in a frying pan, add 250 g (8 oz) minced lamb and cook for 10 minutes until browned. Stir in 2 finely chopped garlic cloves and 1 teaspoon sweet smoked paprika and cook for 30 seconds. Add 150 ml (¼ pint) passata and 1 thyme sprig and simmer for 10–15 minutes until thickened and most of the liquid has evaporated. Scoop out some of the flesh from the aubergines, leaving behind the shells. Chop the flesh and add to the lamb mixture, then spoon into the shells. Scatter over 50 g (2 oz) each of grated mozzarella and Manchego cheese. Bake in the oven for 5–10 minutes until the cheese melts.

chorizo in red wine

Serves **4–6**
Preparation time **5 minutes**
Cooking time **8–10 minutes**

1 tablespoon **olive oil**
250 g (8 oz) **chorizo**
  sausage, thickly sliced
125 ml (4 fl oz) **fruity red wine**

Heat the oil in a large frying pan, add the chorizo and fry for 1–2 minutes on each side until golden and the natural oil has been released.

Pour in the wine and cook for a further 5 minutes until syrupy, then serve with plenty of bread for mopping up the juices.

For chorizo with lentils & wine, fry the chorizo as above, then remove from the pan. Add 1 finely chopped onion to the pan and cook for 5 minutes until softened. Stir in 150 g (5 oz) Puy lentils and the red wine as above and simmer for a couple of minutes. Add 500 ml (17 fl oz) hot chicken stock, return the chorizo to the pan and simmer for 25 minutes or until most of the liquid has been absorbed and the lentils are tender. Scatter with chopped parsley and serve.

saffron & almond chicken

Serves **4–6**
Preparation time **15 minutes**,
    plus infusing and cooling
Cooking time **30 minutes**

pinch of **saffron threads**
2 tablespoons **boiling water**
4 tablespoons **olive oil**
2 **garlic cloves**, peeled
1 slice of **white bread**, crusts
    removed and torn into
    chunks
50 g (2 oz) **blanched
    almonds**
1 **onion**, chopped
125 ml (4 fl oz) **dry white
    wine**
75 ml (3 fl oz) **chicken stock**
1 **bay leaf**
squeeze of **lemon juice**,
    to taste
4 boneless, skinless **chicken
    breasts**, about 125 g (4 oz)
    each, thickly sliced
salt and **pepper**

To garnish
toasted **flaked almonds**
chopped **parsley**

Place the saffron in a small heatproof bowl and pour over the measurement water. Leave to infuse. Meanwhile, heat 1 tablespoon of the oil in a large frying pan, add the garlic, bread and almonds and cook for 2–3 minutes, stirring, until golden. Remove from the pan and set aside.

Heat another 1 tablespoon of the oil in the pan, add the onion and cook for 5–7 minutes until very soft and golden. Add the wine, stock, bay leaf and saffron water, then season and simmer for 10 minutes until most of the liquid has evaporated. Leave to cool slightly.

Place the reserved almond mixture in a food processor or blender and add the cooled onion and cooking liquid, discarding the bay leaf. Blend to a smooth sauce, adding lemon juice to taste. Keep warm.

Rub the remaining oil over the chicken and season well. Heat a griddle pan until smoking hot, then add the chicken and cook for 10 minutes, turning occasionally, until charred and cooked through. Pile up the chicken on a plate and spoon over the sauce. Served scattered with toasted flaked almonds and chopped parsley.

For saffron chicken skewers, cut the chicken breasts into bite-sized pieces. Pour 1 tablespoon boiling water over the saffron threads and leave to infuse for 10 minutes, then stir together with ½ teaspoon hot smoked paprika and 2 tablespoons olive oil and season well. Toss together with the chicken, then thread on to 12 metal skewers. Cook in a preheated hot griddle for 10 minutes, turning frequently, until the chicken is charred and cooked through. Squeeze over a little lemon juice and serve scattered with toasted flaked almonds.

crispy ham bites

Serves **8**
Preparation **10 minutes**,
  plus standing
Cooking time **10 minutes**

8 slices of **bread**
4 large slices of **ham**
250 ml (8 fl oz) **milk**
2 **eggs**, beaten
5 tablespoons **olive oil**
½ teaspoon **hot smoked
  paprika**

Make 4 sandwiches with the bread slices and ham,
then dip them in the milk. Place on a plate and lightly
weigh down with another plate. Leave for 15 minutes.

Place the eggs in a shallow bowl and dip the sandwiches
into the egg. Heat a little of the oil in a frying pan, add
the sandwiches in batches and cook for 3–5 minutes
until golden all over, adding more oil as necessary.

Cut into quarters, then transfer to serving plates and
serve sprinkled with the paprika.

For crispy cheese bites, mix together 100 g (3½ oz)
grated mozzarella cheese and 75 g (3 oz) grated
Manchego cheese. Sandwich together with the bread
and then continue as above, omitting the paprika.

pork empanadillas

Makes **8**
Preparation time **15 minutes**,
  plus cooling
Cooking time **35 minutes**

3 tablespoons **olive oil**
250 g (8 oz) **minced pork**
1 **onion**, finely chopped
2 **garlic cloves**, crushed
3 **tomatoes**, roughly chopped
2 teaspoons **tomato purée**
1 teaspoon **hot smoked
  paprika**
1 **ready-roasted red pepper**
  from a jar, drained and
  chopped
500 g (1 lb) pack **puff pastry**
beaten **egg yolk**, to glaze
salt and **pepper**

Heat half the oil in a frying pan, add the pork, season
and fry for 5 minutes, breaking up the clumps, until
browned. Remove from the pan and set aside.

Add the remaining oil and onion to the pan and cook
for 5 minutes until softened, then add the garlic and
cook for 30 seconds. Add the tomatoes, tomato purée
and paprika and cook for a further 5 minutes until pulpy.
Return the pork to the pan with the pepper, stir through
and continue to cook for 10–12 minutes, then leave
to cool.

Roll out the pastry on a lightly floured work surface until
about 5 mm (¼ inch) thick. Using a small plate, cut out
8 x 15 cm (6 inch) circles, rerolling the trimmings as
necessary. Spoon a little of the pork mixture on to one
half of each circle. Brush around the edges with the
egg yolk. Fold over the pastry, press out any air and
then seal the edges with a fork. Brush with more egg.

Place the pastries on a large baking sheet and bake
in a preheated oven, 200°C (400°F), Gas Mark 6, for
15 minutes or until golden and crisp.

For tuna & chorizo empanadillas, replace the minced
pork with 150 g (5 oz) finely chopped chorizo sausage
and fry as above until lightly browned, then remove from
the pan. Continue as above, adding the cooked chorizo
and a drained 200 g (7 oz) can tuna in spring water with
the roasted pepper.

lamb cutlets with quince aioli

Serves **6**

Preparation time **10 minutes**,
  plus cooling

Cooking time **45–50 minutes**

300 g (10 oz) **quinces**
3 **garlic cloves**, crushed
4 tablespoons **olive oil**
400 g (13 oz) **mayonnaise**
18 **lamb cutlets**
salt and **pepper**
chopped **parsley**, for garnish

Place the quinces in a saucepan and cover with cold water. Bring to the boil, then reduce the heat and simmer for 30 minutes or until soft. Drain and leave to cool. When cool enough to handle, cut each quince in half and remove the core, then peel and place in a large bowl.

Mash to a smooth purée, then stir in the garlic, 3 tablespoons of the oil and the mayonnaise until well combined. Season with salt and pepper.

Rub the remaining oil over the lamb and season well. Heat a griddle pan until smoking hot, then add the lamb and cook for 5–7 minutes on each side until charred and just pink in the centre. Serve with the quince aioli scattered with chopped parsley.

For lamb & quince stew, heat 1 tablespoon olive oil in a heavy-based pan, add 500 g (1 lb) stewing lamb and cook for 5 minutes until browned all over. Remove from the pan and set aside. Add a little more oil to the pan if needed, add 1 sliced onion and cook for 5 minutes until softened. Stir in 2 chopped garlic cloves, 1 teaspoon hot smoked paprika and a cinnamon stick. Pour in 300 ml (½ pint) lamb or chicken stock and bring to the boil. Reduce the heat and simmer for 30 minutes, adding a little water if necessary. Add 1 peeled, cored and chopped quince and simmer for a further 30 minutes until the quince is soft and the lamb is cooked through.

paprika chicken wings & garlic

Serves **6–8**
Preparation time **10 minutes**
Cooking time **1 hour**

1 kg (2 lb) **chicken wings**
2 tablespoons **hot smoked paprika**
5 tablespoons **olive oil**
1 **garlic bulb**, cloves
    separated and lightly bruised
2 **thyme sprigs**
125 ml (4 fl oz) **sweet sherry**
salt and **pepper**

Toss together the chicken wings, paprika, oil and garlic cloves in a large bowl and season well. Tip into a shallow roasting tin and scatter with the thyme. Roast in a preheated oven, 200°C (400°F), Gas Mark 6, for 30 minutes.

Turn the wings over and pour in the sherry. Return to the oven and cook for a further 30 minutes or until the chicken is cooked through.

Transfer the chicken to a serving dish, squeeze the garlic from their skins, drizzle over the cooking juices and serve.

For garlic chicken & bean stew, replace the chicken wings with 12 chicken drumsticks. Heat 2 tablespoons olive oil in a heavy-based frying pan, add the chicken and cook for 5–10 minutes until golden all over, then remove from the pan and set aside. Add 1 chopped onion to the pan and cook for 5 minutes until softened. Add the garlic bulb, separated into cloves, and stir around the pan. Replace the sweet sherry with 125 ml (4 fl oz) dry sherry, pour over and simmer for a couple of minutes until reduced by half. Return the chicken to the pan, pour over 150 ml (5 fl oz) chicken stock and add the thyme sprigs. Simmer for 30 minutes, then add a rinsed and drained 400 g (13 oz) can cannellini beans and cook for a further 10 minutes until the chicken is cooked through. Sprinkle over a little sweet smoked paprika and serve.

moorish skewers

Serves **4–6**

Preparation time **15 minutes**, plus marinating

Cooking time **10 minutes**

2 teaspoons **cumin seeds**

2 teaspoons **coriander seeds**

2 teaspoons **fennel seeds**

1 teaspoon **sweet smoked paprika**

squeeze of **lemon juice**

3 tablespoons **olive oil**

2 **garlic cloves**, crushed

handful of **parsley**, chopped, plus extra to garnish

500 g (1 lb) **pork fillet**, cubed

salt and **pepper**

Place the spice seeds in a spice grinder and crush to a fine powder. Alternatively, use a pestle and mortar. Tip into a bowl and mix together with the paprika, lemon juice, oil, garlic and parsley, then season with salt and pepper.

Add the pork and stir until well coated. Cover and leave to marinate in the refrigerator for at least 2 hours and preferably overnight.

Thread the pork on to 15 metal skewers. Heat a griddle pan until smoking hot, then add the skewers and cook for 10 minutes, turning frequently, until charred and just cooked through. Serve immediately scattered with extra parsley.

For Moorish chicken, make the marinade as above. Replace the pork with 8 chicken thighs and rub the marinade all over. Cover and leave to marinate in the refrigerator as above. Transfer the chicken to an ovenproof dish and bake in a preheated oven, 190°C (375°F), Gas Mark 5, for 45 minutes or until golden and cooked through.

serrano ham, fig & rocket salad

Serves **4–6**
Preparation time **10 minutes**

100 g (3½ oz) **rocket leaves**
4 **figs**, halved or quartered
　if large
150 g (5 oz) **Serrano ham**,
　sliced

Dressing
1 tablespoon finely chopped
　shallot
1 **thyme sprig**, leaves stripped
　and finely chopped
1 tablespoon **sherry vinegar**
3 tablespoons **extra virgin
　olive oil**
salt and **pepper**

Make the dressing. Mix together the shallot, thyme and vinegar in a bowl. Season well, then whisk in the oil until well combined.

Toss the rocket with a little of the dressing, then arrange on a serving plate with the figs and ham. Drizzle over the remaining dressing and serve.

For ham & goats' cheese baked figs, cut a cross into the top of each of 8 large figs using a sharp knife, making sure not to cut the whole way through. Place a small spoonful of soft goats' cheese in the centre of each fig. Wrap 1 slice of Serrano ham around each fig and secure with a cocktail stick if necessary. Place in an ovenproof dish and drizzle with a little olive oil. Bake in a preheated oven, 200°C (400°F), Gas Mark 6, for 10–15 minutes until the ham is crisp. Drizzle with a little sherry vinegar and olive oil and serve.

morcilla with broad beans

Serves **4–6**
Preparation time **10 minutes**
Cooking time **7–10 minutes**

2 tablespoons **olive oil**
150 g (5 oz) **morcilla** or **black pudding**, thickly sliced
6 **spring onions**, sliced
3 **garlic cloves**, thinly sliced
½ teaspoon **fennel seeds**
500 g (1 lb) podded **broad beans**
125 ml (4 fl oz) **chicken stock**
handful of **mint leaves**, chopped, plus extra to garnish
salt and **pepper**

Heat the oil in a frying pan, add the morcilla or black pudding and cook for 1–2 minutes until crisp all over. Remove from the pan and set aside.

Add the spring onions, garlic and fennel seeds to the pan and cook for 30 seconds. Stir in the broad beans and stock, season and cook for 3–5 minutes until the beans are just cooked through.

Return the morcilla or black pudding to the pan, add the mint and heat through. Scatter with extra mint and serve with crusty bread.

For broad beans with chorizo & tomatoes, replace the morcilla with 125 g (4 oz) thickly sliced chorizo sausage and cook in the oil for 2 minutes until golden and crisp. Omit the spring onions and fennel seeds. Add the garlic and 1 teaspoon tomato purée and cook for 30 seconds, then add the broad beans, 2 chopped tomatoes and the stock and continue to cook as above, omitting the mint. Serve scattered with chopped parsley.

ham croquettes

Serves **8**

Preparation time **20 minutes**, plus chilling

Cooking time **25 minutes**

75 g (3 oz) **butter**
½ **onion**, finely chopped
200 g (7 oz) **Serrano ham**, chopped
200 g (7 oz) **plain flour**
500 ml (17 fl oz) **milk**
2 **eggs**, beaten
200 g (7 oz) **dried white breadcrumbs**
vegetable oil, for deep-frying
salt and **pepper**

Heat the butter in a large saucepan, add the onion and cook for 5 minutes until softened. Add the ham and cook for 1 minute.

Stir in 125 g (4 oz) of the flour and cook for 1 minute. Gradually add the milk, beating well between each addition. Bring to the boil, then reduce the heat and cook gently for 5 minutes until thickened. Season and then pour into a bowl. Press a sheet of clingfilm over the surface and then chill for at least 6 hours or preferably overnight.

Roll walnut-sized pieces of the ham mixture into tapered cylinders using lightly oiled hands. Leave to rest in the refrigerator for 30 minutes. Place the remaining flour on a plate, the eggs in a shallow bowl and the breadcrumbs on a separate plate. Dust each croquette in the flour, then roll in the egg and finally in the breadcrumbs, shaking off any excess each time.

Pour the oil into a large, deep saucepan or deep fat-fryer to a depth of at least 7 cm (3 inches) and heat to 180–190°C (350–375°F), or until a cube of bread browns in 30 seconds. Deep-fry the croquettes in batches for about 3 minutes until golden, then remove with a slotted spoon. Drain on kitchen paper and keep warm while you cook the remaining croquettes.

For chicken & egg croquettes with matzo coating,

cook the onion as above. Omit the ham, then make the white sauce. When thickened, stir in 100 g (3½ oz) cooled cooked chicken breast, 1 chopped hard-boiled egg, a pinch of paprika and a handful of chopped parsley. Leave to cool and chill as above. Coat the croquettes as above, replacing the dried breadcrumbs with 150 g (5 oz) medium matzo meal. Deep-fry as above.

132

chicken & two-bean paella

Serves **6**
Preparation time **10 minutes**,
   plus standing
Cooking time **30–35 minutes**

4 tablespoons **olive oil**
6 boneless, skinless **chicken
   thighs**, 550 g (1 ⅛ lb) total
   weight, cut into chunks
1 **onion**, finely chopped
3 **garlic cloves**, chopped
1 teaspoon **sweet smoked
   paprika**
1 **tomato**, chopped
pinch of **saffron threads**
1 **rosemary sprig**
1.2 litres (2 pints) **chicken
   stock**
500 g (1 lb) **paella rice**
250 g (8 oz) **fine green
   beans**, trimmed
200 g (7 oz) can **butter
   beans**, rinsed and drained
salt and **pepper**

Heat half the oil in a large, deep frying pan or paella
pan, add the chicken and cook for 5–10 minutes
until well browned all over. Remove from the pan and
set aside.

Add the remaining oil to the pan, stir in the onion and
cook for 5 minutes until softened. Add the garlic
and paprika and cook for a further 30 seconds.
Return the chicken to the pan with the tomato and
cook for a couple of minutes until the tomato is pulpy.

Stir in the saffron, rosemary and stock and bring to the
boil, then reduce to a simmer, add the rice and beans
and stir well. Cook for 15 minutes, adding more water
if necessary, until the liquid has been absorbed and the
rice is tender. Turn off the heat, cover the pan and leave
to stand for 5 minutes, then serve immediately.

For chicken & bean stew, heat 1 tablespoon olive
oil in a heavy-based saucepan, add 6 boneless,
skinless chicken thighs, cut into chunks, and cook for
5–10 minutes until golden. Remove from the pan and
set aside. Heat 2 tablespoons olive oil in the pan, stir
in 1 sliced onion and cook for 7 minutes until softened.
Add 2 sliced garlic cloves and 1 teaspoon each of
tomato purée and hot smoked paprika and cook for
a further 30 seconds, then stir in a 400 g (13 oz) can
chopped tomatoes. Return the chicken to the pan
and simmer for 20 minutes or until cooked through.
Add 200 g (7 oz) rinsed and drained canned cannellini
beans and a handful of chopped kale and continue to
cook for a further 5 minutes until piping hot. Serve with
plenty of crusty bread.

pork & tomato rice pot

Serves **4**
Preparation time **10 minutes**
Cooking time **25–30 minutes**

3 tablespoons **olive oil**
300 g (10 oz) **pork fillet**,
  sliced
1 **onion**, finely chopped
3 **garlic cloves**, finely chopped
250 g (8 oz) **paella rice**
2 teaspoons **smoked paprika**
200 g (7 oz) can **chopped
  tomatoes**
650 ml (1 pint 2 fl oz) **hot
  chicken stock**
125 g (4 oz) **baby spinach
  leaves**
salt and **pepper**
lemon wedges, to serve

Heat 1 tablespoon of the oil in a large, deep frying pan over a high heat, add the pork and cook for 3 minutes until golden and almost cooked through. Remove from the pan and set aside.

Add the remaining oil to the pan, reduce the heat and cook the onion for 3 minutes until softened, then stir in the garlic and cook for a further 30 seconds. Add the rice and cook for 1 minute, then add the paprika and tomatoes.

Bring to the boil, then reduce the heat and simmer for 2–3 minutes. Pour in the stock, season with salt and pepper and cook for a further 12–15 minutes until most of the liquid has been absorbed.

Fork the spinach through the rice, arrange the pork on top, then cover and continue to cook for 3–4 minutes until cooked through. Serve with lemon wedges for squeezing over.

For chorizo, tomato & rice soup, heat 2 tablespoons olive oil in a large, heavy-based saucepan, add 125 g (4 oz) thickly sliced chorizo sausage and cook for 2–3 minutes until golden, then add 1 sliced garlic clove. Pour in a 400 g (13 oz) can chopped tomatoes and 1 litre (1¾ pints) hot vegetable stock. Add a pinch of sugar, season with salt and pepper and simmer for 10 minutes. Stir in 250 g (8 oz) ready-cooked rice and 100 g (3½ oz) rocket leaves, heat through until piping hot and serve.

red pepper & paprika pork

Serves **6–8**
Preparation time **15 minutes**
Cooking time **20–25 minutes**

2 **garlic cloves**, crushed
2 **ready-roasted red peppers**
   from a jar, drained and
   chopped
1 teaspoon **sweet smoked**
   paprika
1 **thyme sprig**, leaves stripped
   and chopped, plus extra
   sprigs to garnish
3 tablespoons **olive oil**
2 **pork tenderloins**, about
   500 g (1 lb) each
salt and **pepper**

Mix together the garlic, red peppers, paprika, thyme and 2 tablespoons of the oil in a bowl, then season well.

Lay the pork tenderloins on a chopping board, then, using a sharp knife, slice through lengthways and open out like a book. Scatter the red pepper mixture over the pork and then tightly roll up and secure with cocktail sticks.

Place the pork in a lightly greased shallow roasting tray, season with salt and pepper and drizzle over the remaining oil. Roast in a preheated oven, 200°C (400°F), Gas Mark 6, for 20–25 minutes until golden and cooked through.

Cut into bite-sized pieces and serve scattered with thyme springs to garnish.

For grilled pork chops & red peppers, place 6 pork chops, 3 cored, deseeded and thickly sliced red peppers, 6 unpeeled garlic cloves and 2 thyme sprigs in a lightly greased flameproof dish. Mix together 1 teaspoon sweet smoked paprika and 2 tablespoons olive oil, then drizzle over the pork and peppers and season. Cook under a preheated hot grill for 10 minutes, then turn the chops and peppers over and cook for a further 5–10 minutes until the pork is charred and cooked through.

ham & artichoke gratin

Serves **4–6**

Preparation time **10 minutes**

Cooking time **15–25 minutes**

25 g (1 oz) **butter**

25 g (1 oz) **plain flour**

300 ml (½ pint) **milk**

12 **ready-cooked artichoke hearts**, quartered

150 g (5 oz) **smoked jamón** or other **ham**, chopped

50 g (2 oz) **Manchego cheese**, grated

pinch of **sweet smoked paprika**

salt and **pepper**

Heat the butter in a medium saucepan, then stir in the flour until well combined. Cook for 2 minutes, then gradually add the milk, beating well between each addition. Bring to the boil, then reduce the heat and simmer for about 5–10 minutes until the sauce thickens and coats the back of a wooden spoon. Season with salt and pepper.

Add the artichokes and ham to the sauce and gently stir together. Spoon into 1 lightly greased medium gratin dish or 4 lightly greased individual ramekins. Scatter over the cheese and sprinkle with the paprika.

Cook under a preheated hot grill for 5–10 minutes until browned and bubbling.

For ham, potato & artichoke gratin, place 625 g (1¼ lb) peeled and thinly sliced potatoes, the artichoke hearts as above and 125 g (4 oz) thickly sliced ham in a lightly greased gratin dish. Heat together 125 ml (4 fl oz) vegetable stock, 150 ml (¼ pint) each of double cream and milk and 1 crushed garlic clove until nearly boiling. Pour over the gratin, then sprinkle over 50 g (2 oz) grated Gruyère cheese. Cover with foil and bake in a preheated oven, 180°C (350°F), Gas Mark 4, for 30 minutes. Remove the foil and cook for a further 30 minutes or until the potatoes are tender and the gratin is golden.

cheat's chicken & chorizo paella

Serves **4**

Preparation time **20 minutes**

Cooking time **25–30 minutes**

2 tablespoons **olive oil**

1 large **onion**, roughly
chopped

150 g (5 oz) **chorizo
sausage**, diced

2 **garlic cloves**, finely chopped

1 **red pepper**, cored,
deseeded and diced

1 **orange pepper**, cored,
deseeded and diced

4 **tomatoes**, diced

200 g (7 oz) **white long-grain
rice**

large pinch of **smoked
paprika**

large pinch of **saffron threads**

125–200 g (4–7 oz) **cooked
chicken**, diced

600–750 ml (1–1¼ pints)
chicken stock

100 g (3½ oz) **frozen peas**

75 g (3 oz) **marinated mixed
olives**

3 tablespoons chopped
parsley, to garnish (optional)

lemon wedges, to serve

Heat the oil in a large frying pan, add the onion and chorizo and fry, stirring, until the onion is pale golden. Stir in the garlic, peppers and tomatoes and cook for 2–3 minutes until just softened.

Stir in the rice, then mix in the paprika, saffron, chicken and about half the stock. Bring to the boil, stirring, then cover, reduce the heat and simmer for about 20 minutes until the rice is tender, adding the remaining stock if necessary. Stir in the peas and olives and cook until the peas are tender. Serve scattered with the parsley, if liked, and lemon wedges for squeezing over.

For chicken jambalaya, fry the onion in the oil as above with 150 g (5 oz) chopped smoked back bacon. Add the garlic, peppers and tomatoes, then mix in the rice. Replace the paprika and saffron with 1 teaspoon Cajun spice mix. Add the chicken and stock and simmer until tender. Omit the olives and add 100 g (3½ oz) sliced okra with the peas, thn ook until tender.

spanish-style terrine

Serves **8**
Preparation time **30 minutes**,
    plus cooling and chilling
Cooking time **1 hour**
    20 minutes

20 slices of **Serrano ham**
2 tablespoons **olive oil**
1 **onion**, finely chopped
2 **garlic cloves**, crushed
75 ml (3 fl oz) **Fino sherry**
500 g (1 lb) **minced pork**
handful of **thyme sprigs**,
    leaves stripped and chopped
2 boneless, skinless **chicken
    breasts**, 250 g (8 oz) total
    weight, each thinly sliced
    lengthways into 5 pieces
salt and **pepper**

Line a 9 x 17 cm (3½ x 6¾ inch) terrine or loaf tin with the Serrano ham, leaving plenty of overhang so that the terrine can be completely enclosed, then chop the remaining slices.

Heat the oil in a frying pan, add the onion and chopped ham and cook for 5 minutes until the onion is softened. Add the garlic and cook for a further 30 seconds, then pour in the sherry and cook until evaporated. Transfer to a bowl and leave to cool, then mix together with the pork and thyme and season well.

Spoon half the pork mixture into the terrine, pressing down firmly. Arrange the chicken slices on top, ensuring the pork is completely covered. Top with the remaining pork and press down well, then cover with the ham.

Cover with foil and place in a deep roasting tin. Pour in boiling water to come halfway up the sides of the tin. Place in a preheated oven, 180°C (350°F), Gas Mark 4, for 1 hour until the juices run clear.

Leave to cool slightly, then drain away any juices from the terrine. Cover the top with foil, then cut out a piece of cardboard and fit on top. Weigh down with heavy cans and chill overnight. Bring up to room temperature, remove the cans, cardboard and foil and then turn out on to a serving plate. Cut into thick slices and serve with Spanish Tomato Salad (see below), if liked.

For Spanish tomato salad, to serve as an accompaniment, whisk together 1 tablespoon sherry vinegar, 1 teaspoon sweet smoked paprika, 3 tablespoons olive oil and 1 thyme sprig, leaves stripped and chopped. Roughly chop 5 tomatoes and stir through the dressing, then season.

chorizo & red pepper stew

Serves **4**
Preparation time **5 minutes**
Cooking time **25 minutes**

500 g (1 lb) **new potatoes**
1 teaspoon **olive oil**
2 **red onions**, chopped
2 **red peppers**, cored,
    deseeded and chopped
100 g (3½ oz) **chorizo**
    sausage, thinly sliced
500 g (1 lb) **plum tomatoes**,
    chopped, or a 400 g (13 oz)
    can **tomatoes**, drained
400 g (13 oz) can **chickpeas**,
    rinsed and drained
2 tablespoons chopped
    parsley, to garnish

Cook the potatoes in a saucepan of boiling water for 12–15 minutes until tender. Drain, then slice.

Meanwhile, heat the oil in a large frying pan, add the onions and red peppers and fry for 3–4 minutes until beginning to soften. Add the chorizo and cook for a further 2 minutes.

Add the potato slices, tomatoes and chickpeas and bring to the boil, then reduce the heat and simmer for 10 minutes. Scatter over the parsley and serve with some crusty bread to mop up all the juices.

tortilla pizza with salami

Makes **2**
Preparation time **5 minutes**
Cooking time **8–10 minutes**

2 large **flour tortillas** or
  flatbreads
4 tablespoons **ready-made**
  tomato pasta sauce
100 g (3½ oz) **spicy salami**
  slices
150 g (5 oz) **mozzarella**
  cheese, thinly sliced
1 tablespoon **oregano leaves**,
  plus extra to garnish
salt and **pepper**

Lay the tortillas or flatbreads on 2 large baking sheets. Top each with half the pasta sauce, spreading it up to the edge. Arrange the salami and mozzarella slices and oregano leaves over the tops.

Bake in a preheated oven, 200°C (400°F), Gas Mark 6, for 8–10 minutes or until the cheese has melted and is golden. Serve scattered with extra oregano leaves.

For spicy salami, mozzarella & tomato quesadilla,

lay 1 large flour tortilla or flatbread on the work surface. Top with 2 tablespoons tomato pasta sauce, 50 g (2 oz) salami slices, 75 g (3 oz) diced mozzarella cheese and a few basil leaves. Add a second tortilla and press flat. Heat a large frying pan or griddle pan until hot, add the quesadilla and cook for 2–3 minutes on each side. Cut into wedges to serve.

chicken & rice bake

Serves **4**

Preparation time **15 minutes**

Cooking time **1 hour**

8 boneless, skinless **chicken thighs**, about 750 g (1½ lb) total weight

8 **streaky bacon rashers**, rind removed

2 tablespoons **olive oil**

250 g (8 oz) **white long-grain rice**

1 **onion**, chopped

2 **garlic cloves**, crushed

1 teaspoon **ground turmeric**

grated rind and juice of ½ **lemon**

500 ml (17 fl oz) **hot chicken stock**

1 tablespoon chopped **fresh coriander**

salt and **pepper**

Wrap each chicken thigh with a bacon rasher and secure in place with a cocktail stick.

Heat the oil in a flameproof casserole, add the chicken and cook over a high heat for 5 minutes until browned all over. Remove from the pan and set aside.

Add the rice to the pan and cook over a low heat, stirring, for 1 minute. Add the onion, garlic, turmeric, lemon rind, stock and salt and pepper. Arrange the chicken thighs over the rice, pressing down gently.

Cover with a layer of foil, then the lid. Transfer to a preheated oven, 180°C (350°F), Gas Mark 4, and bake for 50 minutes or until the chicken is cooked through and the rice is tender.

Stir in the coriander and lemon juice. Discard the cocktail sticks and serve with Tangy Yogurt Sauce (see below).

For tangy yogurt sauce, to serve as an accompaniment, mix together 150 g (5 oz) Greek yogurt, 1 teaspoon grated lemon rind, 1 crushed garlic clove, 2 teaspoons lemon juice and 1 tablespoon chopped parsley in a bowl, then season with salt and pepper.

chorizo, pepper & oregano salad

Serves **2–4**
Preparation time **15 minutes**,
  plus cooling
Cooking time **10 minutes**

1 tablespoon **olive oil**
2 **red peppers**, cored,
  deseeded and cut into
  2 cm (¾ inch) pieces
2 **yellow peppers**, cored,
  deseeded and cut into
  2 cm (¾ inch) pieces
200 g (7 oz) **chorizo
  sausage**, sliced
1 **red onion**, finely diced
2 tablespoons **sherry vinegar**
½ bunch of **oregano**, roughly
  chopped
75 g (3 oz) **rocket leaves**
salt and **pepper**

Heat the oil in a large frying pan over a high heat, add the peppers and cook for 2–3 minutes until they start to colour. Add the chorizo and fry for a further 3 minutes, then reduce the heat to low, add the onion and cook for a further 3 minutes. Deglaze the pan with the vinegar and cook for 1 minute to reduce.

Transfer the pepper mixture to a large salad bowl and leave to cool slightly, then toss with the oregano and rocket. Season with salt and pepper and serve with Spicy Romesco Sauce (see below).

For spicy romesco sauce, to serve as an accompaniment, soak 1 dried ranchero chilli in water for 1 hour, then drain. Place 4 ready-marinated red peppers, the ranchero chilli, 2 skinned and deseeded tomatoes, 20 g (¾ oz) each of toasted blanched almonds and roasted hazelnuts, 1 garlic clove, 1 tablespoon red wine vinegar and 1 teaspoon smoked paprika in a food processor or blender and blend briefly until it forms a smooth sauce. Season with salt and pepper.

vegetables

spinach, tomato & egg tarts

Serves **6**
Preparation time **10 minutes**
Cooking time **20 minutes**

3 tablespoons **olive oil**
3 **garlic cloves**, finely chopped
½ teaspoon **hot smoked**
  paprika
200 g (7 oz) can **chopped**
  tomatoes
200 g (7 oz) **baby spinach**
  leaves
6 **individual ready-made**
  savoury tart cases, each
  8 cm (3¼ in) in diameter
6 **eggs**
100 g (3½ oz) **Manchego**
  cheese, grated
salt and **pepper**

Heat half the oil in a saucepan, add the garlic and cook for 30 seconds, then stir in the paprika. Add the tomatoes and a little water if necessary and simmer for 10 minutes until most of the liquid has evaporated and the mixture has thickened, then season.

Place the spinach in a large colander and pour over boiling water until wilted. Leave to cool slightly, then squeeze out any excess water and roughly chop.

Arrange the tart cases on a baking sheet. Divide the spinach between the pastry cases, then spoon a little of the tomato sauce over each one. Break 1 egg on top of each, sprinkle with the cheese and then drizzle over the remaining oil. Bake in a preheated oven, 200°C (400°F), Gas Mark 6, for 10 minutes or until the eggs are cooked to your liking.

For homemade pastry cases, place 175 g (6 oz) plain flour and 75 g (3 oz) cubed cold butter in a food processor and whizz until the mixture resembles fine breadcrumbs. Stir in about 3 tablespoons cold water until the mixture just comes together. Wrap the dough in clingfilm and chill for 30 minutes. Roll out the pastry on a lightly floured work surface until 5 mm (¼ inch) thick and stamp out 6 rounds, big enough to fit inside 8 cm (3¼ in) diameter individual tart tins, rerolling the trimmings if necessary. Line the tins with the pastry and trim off the excess. Line the cases with baking paper and fill with baking beans. Bake in a preheated oven, 200°C (400°F), Gas Mark 6, for 7 minutes. Remove the paper and beans, then return to the oven and cook for a further 5 minutes until crisp and golden.

cinnamon mushroom skewers

Serves **4**
Preparation time **5 minutes**
Cooking time **4–6 minutes**

finely grated rind of **1 lemon**
½ teaspoon **ground cinnamon**
1 **garlic clove**, crushed
3 tablespoons **olive oil**
250 g (8 oz) large **mixed mushrooms**, trimmed
squeeze of **lemon juice**
salt and **pepper**
chopped **parsley**, to garnish

Mix together most of the lemon rind (saving some for garnish) with the cinnamon, garlic and oil in a small bowl. Thread the mushrooms on to 12 metal skewers, then brush all over with the flavoured oil and season well.

Heat a griddle pan until smoking hot, then add the mushroom skewers and cook for 2–3 minutes on each side until charred and just tender.

Squeeze over a little lemon juice, then scatter with chopped parsley and the remaining lemon rind and serve.

For marinated mushrooms, stir together 150 ml (¼ pint) olive oil, the juice of ½ lemon, a pinch each of ground cinnamon and dried chilli flakes and 1 thyme sprig. Place the mixed mushrooms as above in a non-metallic bowl and pour over the marinade. Cover and leave to marinate in the refrigerator for at least 3 hours before serving.

creamy white gazpacho soup

Serves **4–6**

Preparation time **10 minutes**, plus soaking and chilling

125 g (4 oz) **slightly stale white bread**, crusts removed

900 ml (1½ pints) **iced water**

200 g (7 oz) **blanched almonds**

3 **garlic cloves**, crushed

5 tablespoons **extra virgin olive oil**, plus extra for drizzling

salt and **pepper**

handful of **seedless white grapes**, halved, to serve

Place the bread in a dish and pour over half the measurement water, then leave to soak for 20 minutes.

Put the almonds and garlic in a food processor and pulse until very finely chopped. Add the bread with its soaking liquid and the oil and blend until smooth. Season with salt and pepper, then gradually blend in the remaining measurement water until the consistency of single cream.

Chill for at least 2 hours, then ladle into bowls, scatter with the grapes and serve drizzled with a little extra olive oil.

For Spanish almond & onion soup, heat 1 tablespoon olive oil and 15 g (2 oz) butter in a frying pan, add 5 sliced onions and cook over a low heat for 20–25 minutes until very soft. Add 1 sliced garlic clove and cook for a further 2 minutes. Stir in 25 g (1 oz) ground almonds and a pinch of sweet paprika and cook for 2 minutes, then pour in 50 ml (2 fl oz) sherry and leave to bubble away. Pour in 900 ml (1½ pints) hot vegetable stock and simmer for 20 minutes. Ladle into bowls and served sprinkled with grated Manchego cheese.

fried cheese wedges

Serves **6**

Preparation time **15 minutes**

Cooking time **10 minutes**

3 tablespoons **plain flour**

150 g (5 oz) **dried white breadcrumbs**

1 **egg**, beaten

300 g (10 oz) **Manchego cheese**, rind removed and cut into 1 cm (½ inch) wedges

5 tablespoons **olive oil**

sweet paprika, for sprinkling (optional)

salt and **pepper**

Place the flour and breadcrumbs on separate plates and the egg in a shallow bowl. Season the flour with salt and pepper and stir together. Dip the cheese wedges in the flour, then in the egg and finally in the breadcrumbs, shaking off any excess each time.

Heat a little of the oil in a frying pan, add the wedges in batches and fry for about 1 minute on each side until golden. Remove from the pan, drain on kitchen paper and keep warm. Wipe out the pan, discarding any breadcrumbs, and repeat with the remaining wedges.

Serve the wedges hot, sprinkled with paprika, if liked.

For cheese fritters, heat 100 g (3½ oz) butter and 250 ml (8 fl oz) water in a saucepan until the butter has melted. Add 150 g (5 oz) plain flour and a good pinch of sweet paprika and beat until the mixture is smooth and comes away from the sides of the pan. Leave to cool slightly. Gradually beat in 4 eggs, then 125 g (4 oz) grated Manchego cheese. Pour vegetable oil into a large, deep saucepan or deep-fat fryer to a depth of at least 7 cm (3 inches) and heat to 180–190°C (350–375°F), or until a cube of bread browns in 30 seconds. Carefully drop heaped teaspoons of the mixture into the oil in batches, taking care not to overcrowd the pan. Deep-fry the fritters for 5 minutes until golden, then remove with a slotted spoon. Drain on kitchen paper and keep warm while you cook the remaining mixture. Serve hot.

ricotta & red onion tortilla

Serves **1**
Preparation time **10 minutes**
Cooking time **4–5 minutes**

40 g (1½ oz) **ricotta cheese**
½ **red onion**, thinly sliced
1 **tomato**, finely chopped
¼ **green chilli**, deseeded
  and finely chopped
1 tablespoon chopped **fresh
  coriander**
2 **small soft flour tortillas**
olive oil, for brushing

Mix together the ricotta, onion, tomato, chilli and coriander in a bowl.

Heat a griddle pan until hot. Brush the tortillas with a little oil, add to the pan and cook very briefly on each side.

Spread half the ricotta mixture over one half of each tortilla and fold over the other half to cover. Cut in half and serve immediately with a green salad.

spinach with pine nuts & raisins

Serves **6**
Preparation time **5 minutes**,
  plus soaking
Cooking time **10 minutes**

50 g (2 oz) **raisins**
3 tablespoons **olive oil**
400 g (13 oz) **baby spinach
  leaves**
25 g (1 oz) **pine nuts**
2 **garlic cloves**, sliced
3 tablespoons **dry sherry**
salt and **pepper**

Tip the raisins into a heatproof bowl and pour over enough boiling water to cover. Leave to soak for 10 minutes or until plumped up.

Heat 2 tablespoons of the oil in a large frying pan, add the spinach and stir around the pan until just starting to wilt. Remove from the pan and, when cool enough to handle, squeeze away any excess water.

Wipe the pan clean, then add the remaining oil and cook the pine nuts for 1 minute until starting to colour. Add the garlic and cook for a further 1 minute until it starts to change colour.

Pour in the sherry, drain and add the raisins and cook until almost evaporated, then return the spinach to the pan and heat through. Season to taste with salt and pepper and serve.

For spinach, bread & raisin salad, cut 2 slices of baguette into bite-sized pieces, place in a baking tin and toss in a little oil. Bake in a preheated oven, 190°C (375°F), Gas Mark 5, for 5–10 minutes until browned and crisp. Leave to cool. Whisk together 1 tablespoon sherry vinegar, 3 tablespoons olive oil and a pinch of salt in a bowl, then toss together with 200 g (7 oz) mixed spinach and salad leaves and arrange on serving plates with the bread, 25 g (1 oz) raisins and some Manchego cheese shavings.

artichoke & red pepper paella

Serves **4**
Preparation time **10 minutes**
Cooking time **25 minutes**

2 tablespoons **olive oil**
1 **onion**, finely chopped
2 **garlic cloves**, crushed
½ teaspoon **hot smoked
  paprika**
300 g (10 oz) **paella rice**
1 large **ready-roasted red
  pepper** from a jar, sliced
4 **ready-charred artichoke
  hearts**, halved
pinch of **saffron threads**
200 g (7 oz) can **chopped
  tomatoes**
750 ml (1¼ pints) hot
  vegetable stock
salt and **pepper**
chopped **parsley**, to garnish

Heat a large, deep frying pan or paella pan until hot,
then add the oil and onion and cook for 5 minutes until
softened. Stir in the garlic and cook for 30 seconds,
then add the paprika and rice and cook for a further
1 minute, stirring until well coated.

Add the pepper and artichokes, then stir in the saffron
and chopped tomatoes. Pour in the stock and bring to the
boil, then reduce the heat and simmer for 12 minutes or
until most of the liquid has been absorbed.

Stir the rice to evenly distribute the vegetables, then
reduce the heat to very low and cook for 5 minutes
or until all the liquid has been absorbed and the rice
is tender. Season to taste and scatter with chopped
parsley before serving.

For charred artichoke & red pepper salad, toss
1 large red pepper, cored, deseeded and cut into strips,
in a little olive oil. Cook in a preheated smoking hot
griddle pan for 3–5 minutes until lightly charred and
softened. Whisk together ½ teaspoon sweet smoked
paprika, 1 tablespoon sherry vinegar and 3 tablespoons
extra virgin olive oil in a large bowl, then add the
warm red pepper. Rub a little oil over 6 ready-cooked
artichoke hearts and cook in the griddle pan for
2 minutes on each side until charred. Toss with the
pepper, then arrange on serving plates with rocket
leaves tossed in a little of the dressing.

charred leeks with tomato sauce

Serves **4**
Preparation time **10 minutes**
Cooking time **15–17 minutes**

25 g (1 oz) **blanched
  almonds**
150 g (5 oz) **ripe tomatoes**,
  halved
4 tablespoons **olive oil**
1 **garlic clove**, crushed
pinch of **dried chilli flakes**
1 tablespoon **sherry vinegar**
200 g (7 oz) **baby leeks**,
  trimmed and cleaned
salt and **pepper**

Place the almonds in a small, dry frying pan and toast for 5 minutes, shaking the pan frequently, until golden brown. Leave to cool, then roughly chop.

Toss together the tomatoes and 1 teaspoon of the oil, then season. Heat a griddle pan until smoking hot, then add the tomatoes and cook for 3–5 minutes until just charred. Remove from the pan and roughly chop, then toss together with the almonds, garlic, chilli flakes, vinegar and 3 tablespoons of the oil. Season and set aside.

Wipe out the griddle pan, if necessary, then toss the leeks in the remaining oil. Cook in the pan for 7 minutes or until softened and charred. Serve drizzled with the tomato sauce.

For spicy leek & tomato tart, roll out 375 g (12 oz) ready-made shortcrust pastry on a floured work surface and use to line a 23 cm (9 inch) tart tin. Trim off the excess pastry. Line the tart with baking paper and fill with baking beans. Bake in a preheated oven, 190°C (375°F), Gas Mark 5, for 10 minutes. Remove the baking paper and beans, then return to the oven and cook for a further 5 minutes until crisp and golden. Meanwhile, heat a little butter in a frying pan, add 2 trimmed and thinly sliced large leeks, cover and cook over a low heat for 10 minutes until very soft. Stir in 150 g (5 oz) crème fraîche and 25 g (1 oz) grated Parmesan cheese, then season and spoon into the pastry case. Thinly slice 2 tomatoes and arrange on top, then sprinkle over a pinch of hot smoked paprika and drizzle with a little olive oil. Bake in the oven for 10–15 minutes until the tomatoes are soft.

garlic potatoes

Serves **4–6**
Preparation time **10 minutes**
Cooking time **30 minutes**

4 tablespoons **olive oil**
750 g (1 ½ lb) **waxy potatoes**,
   such as Maris Piper, peeled
   and thickly sliced
2 **garlic cloves**, finely chopped
salt and **pepper**
chopped **parsley**, to garnish

Heat the oil in a large, heavy-based frying pan over a medium-high heat, add the potato slices, season with salt and pepper and cook for 5 minutes until starting to turn golden.

Reduce the heat and cook for a further 20 minutes, turning occasionally, until tender and golden all over. Scatter over the garlic and continue to cook for a couple of minutes. Serve scattered with chopped parsley.

For roasted garlic & potato soup, separate 2 garlic heads into cloves and scatter over a roasting tin. Drizzle with 1 tablespoon olive oil and roast in a preheated oven, 120°C (250°F), Gas Mark ½, for 1 ½–2 hours until very soft. Meanwhile, heat 1 tablespoon olive oil in a large saucepan, add 1 chopped onion and cook for 5 minutes until softened, then add 500 g (1 lb) peeled and cubed potatoes and 1 thyme sprig. Pour in 1 litre (1¾ pints) hot vegetable stock and simmer for 15–20 minutes until the potatoes are tender. Remove the thyme and squeeze the garlic flesh out of the skins into the soup. Using a stick blender, purée the soup, then add 100 ml (3½ fl oz) double cream and season before serving.

egg & manchego tortillas

Serves **4**
Preparation time **15 minutes**
Cooking time **20 minutes**

10 **eggs**, beaten
1 **onion**, finely chopped
1 **green chilli**, deseeded and
   finely chopped, plus extra
   to serve
1 **corn on the cob**, kernels
   removed, or 4 tablespoons
   canned sweetcorn
25 g (1 oz) **butter**
75 g (3 oz) **Manchego cheese**,
   crumbled, plus extra
   shavings to serve
1 tablespoon chopped **fresh
   coriander**, plus extra
   to serve
8 **flour tortillas**, warmed
salt and **pepper**
chives, to garnish
4 tablespoons **sweet chilli
   sauce**, to serve (optional)

Place the beaten eggs in a bowl and stir in the
onion, chopped chilli and sweetcorn kernels.
Season well with salt and pepper.

Melt the butter in a large saucepan until foaming.
Add the egg mixture and cook over a medium heat,
stirring constantly, until the eggs are softly scrambled.
Immediately remove the pan from the heat and stir
in the crumbled Manchego and coriander.

Serve immediately on the warmed tortillas, scattered
with green chilli slices, coriander and chives, plus
shavings of Manchego and the sweet chilli sauce or
Homemade Guacamole (see below).

For homemade guacamole, to serve as an alternative
accompaniment, place 1 peeled, stoned and diced
avocado in a food processor or blender with 1 crushed
garlic clove, 1 deseeded and chopped red chilli, the juice
of 1 lime, 1 tablespoon chopped fresh coriander and
salt and pepper. Blend until fairly smooth, then transfer to
a bowl and stir in 1 deseeded and finely chopped tomato.

new potato, bean & tomato salad

Serves **4–6**
Preparation time **10 minutes**
Cooking time **13–15 minutes**

500 g (1 lb) **new potatoes**,
  scrubbed and halved
200 g (7 oz) **green beans**,
  trimmed
2 tablespoons **white wine
  vinegar**
6 tablespoons **extra virgin
  olive oil**
100 g (3½ oz) **cherry
  tomatoes**, halved
handful of **parsley**, chopped
salt and **pepper**

Cook the potatoes in a large saucepan of salted
boiling water for 10 minutes. Add the beans and cook
for a further 3–5 minutes until the vegetables are just
cooked through. Drain well.

Meanwhile, whisk together the vinegar and oil in a
large serving bowl and season well. Stir through the
tomatoes and parsley, then toss through the warm
vegetables. Serve warm or cold.

potatoes with spicy tomato sauce

Serves **6**
Preparation time **10 minutes**
Cooking time **30 minutes**

6 tablespoons **olive oil**
1 **onion**, finely chopped
2 **garlic cloves**, finely chopped
pinch of **dried chilli flakes**
1 teaspoon **hot smoked paprika**
125 ml (4 fl oz) **dry white wine**
400 g (13 oz) can **chopped tomatoes**
pinch of **caster sugar**
1 kg (2 lb) **waxy potatoes**, peeled and quartered
salt and **pepper**

Heat 1 tablespoon of the oil in a heavy-based saucepan, add the onion and cook for 5 minutes until softened. Add the garlic, chilli flakes and paprika and cook for a further 30 seconds.

Pour in the wine and bubble for a couple of minutes until reduced by half. Add the tomatoes and sugar and season with salt and pepper, then cook for 20 minutes, adding a little water if necessary.

Meanwhile, cook the potatoes in a saucepan of boiling water for 5 minutes, then drain well. Heat the remaining oil in a large frying pan, add the potatoes in a single layer (you may have to do this in 2 batches) and cook for 10–15 minutes, turning frequently, until golden and crispy all over.

Transfer the potatoes to a serving bowl and serve with the tomato sauce spooned over.

For spicy tomato-roasted potatoes, mix together 3 tablespoons olive oil, 1 teaspoon tomato purée, 1 teaspoon hot smoked paprika and a pinch of dried thyme in a large bowl. Add 750 g (1½ lb) peeled and cubed potatoes and toss together, then tip into a roasting tin. Roast in a preheated oven, 190°C (375°F), Gas Mark 5, for 45 minutes, turning occasionally, until the potatoes are crisp on the outside and tender inside. Serve scattered with chopped parsley.

courgette & olive flatbreads

Serves **4**
Preparation time **20 minutes**,
  plus rising
Cooking time **15–20 minutes**

150 g (5 oz) packet **pizza
  base mix**
polenta, for sprinkling
1 small **onion**, thinly sliced
2 **garlic cloves**, sliced
2 **courgettes**, thinly sliced
50 g (2 oz) pitted **black olives**
4 tablespoons **extra virgin
  olive oil**, plus extra for
  drizzling
handful of **parsley**, chopped
salt and **pepper**

Make the pizza base dough according to the packet instructions. Divide into 2 pieces and roll out each piece on a lightly floured work surface to an oval shape. Scatter a little polenta over 2 baking sheets, then place the bases on the sheets, cover and leave to rise for 15 minutes.

Place the onion, garlic, courgettes, olives and oil in a bowl and gently toss together, then season well. Scatter the mixture over the bases and drizzle over a little extra oil. Bake in a preheated oven, 200°C (400°F), Gas Mark 6, for 15–20 minutes until crisp. Scatter over the parsley and serve.

For homemade pizza bases, place 250 g (8 oz) strong white bread flour, 1 teaspoon salt and 1 teaspoon fast-action dried yeast in a bowl, then stir in about 175 ml (6 fl oz) warm water and 3 tablespoons extra virgin olive oil to form a soft but not sticky dough. Knead the dough for 5–10 minutes using a dough hook in an electric mixer or on a well-floured surface by hand until smooth. Put the dough in a lightly oiled bowl, cover with a tea towel and leave to rise until doubled in size. Knock back the dough, then divide into 4 and continue as above.

russian salad

Serves **4–6**
Preparation time **15 minutes**
Cooking time **15 minutes**

500 g (1 lb) small **waxy
    potatoes**, scrubbed and
    halved
200 g (7 oz) **baby carrots**,
    scrubbed and halved
125 g (4 oz) **frozen peas**
100 g (3½ oz) **mayonnaise**
1 teaspoon **Dijon mustard**
1 **spring onion**, sliced
2 **cornichons**, sliced
1 teaspoon **capers**, drained
handful of **parsley**, chopped
salt and **pepper**

Cook the potatoes in a large saucepan of salted
boiling water for 10 minutes. Add the carrots and cook
for a further 3 minutes, then add the peas and continue
to cook for 2 minutes until all the vegetables are just
cooked through. Drain, then cool under cold running
water and drain again.

Mix together the mayonnaise and mustard in a large
bowl, then add most of the spring onion, cornichons,
capers and parsley, reserving some for garnish. Stir in
the cooled vegetables, then season with salt and
pepper to taste.

Transfer the salad to a serving bowl and serve
scattered with the reserved ingredients.

For homemade mayonnaise, put 1 egg yolk in a bowl.
Gradually whisk in 125 ml (4 fl oz) olive oil, a drop at a
time, increasing the amount of oil added when it starts
to thicken. Season well and add a squeeze of lemon
juice to taste.

spicy tomato poached eggs

Serves **4**
Preparation time **10 minutes**
Cooking time **25 minutes**

2 tablespoons **olive oil**
1 **onion**, finely chopped
2 **garlic cloves**, crushed
1 teaspoon **sweet smoked paprika**
1 **thyme sprig**
2 x 400 g (13 oz) cans **chopped tomatoes**
200 ml (7 fl oz) **water**
4 **eggs**
salt and **pepper**
chopped **parsley**, to garnish

Heat the oil in a large, deep frying pan, add the onion and cook for 5 minutes until softened. Stir in the garlic and paprika and cook for a further 30 seconds.

Add the thyme sprig, tomatoes and the measurement water, then season with salt and pepper. Bring to the boil, then reduce the heat and simmer for 10 minutes until rich and thickened.

Make 4 small pockets in the tomato sauce, then break an egg into each one. Cover the pan with foil and simmer for about 5 minutes until the egg whites are cooked through. Serve scattered with chopped parsley.

For hearty tomato vegetable stew with eggs, heat 3 tablespoons olive oil in a frying pan, add 1 chopped aubergine and fry until golden. Remove from the pan and set aside. Add 1 cored, deseeded and chopped red pepper and more oil, if needed, to the pan and fry until softened. Remove from the pan and set aside. Make the sauce as above, adding the reserved aubergines and pepper to the pan with the tomatoes. Continue as above.

braised spanish vegetables

Serves **4–6**
Preparation time **10 minutes**
Cooking time **35 minutes**

5 tablespoons **olive oil**
1 **onion**, sliced
2 **garlic cloves**, sliced
200 g (7 oz) can **chopped tomatoes**
1 **green pepper**, cored, deseeded and sliced
1 **aubergine** or 3 **baby aubergines**, sliced
1 **courgette** or 4 **baby courgettes**, sliced
salt and **pepper**

Heat 1 tablespoon of the oil in a large frying pan over a medium heat, add the onion and cook for 5–7 minutes until softened. Stir in the garlic and cook for a further 1 minute. Add the tomatoes and a little water and simmer for 15 minutes.

Meanwhile, heat 1 tablespoon of the oil in a separate frying pan, add the green pepper and cook for 5 minutes, stirring, until softened and lightly browned. Remove from the pan and set aside. Add another 2 tablespoons of the oil to the pan, add the aubergine and cook for 5 minutes until golden, then set aside. Add the remaining oil to the pan, add the courgette and cook for 5 minutes until golden.

Return the pepper and aubergine to the pan, pour over the tomato sauce and season well. Bring to the boil, then reduce the heat and simmer for 10 minutes until the vegetables are very tender and most of the liquid has evaporated.

For summery vegetable flatbreads, prepare the braised vegetables as above and leave to cool. Using a 150 g (5 oz) packet pizza base mix, make the dough according to the packet instructions. Divide into 4 pieces, then roll out each piece on a lightly floured work surface to an oval shape and place on lightly greased baking sheets. Spoon over the braised vegetables and bake in a preheated oven, 200°C (400°F), Gas Mark 6, for 15–20 minutes until crisp.

stuffed artichokes

Serves **4**
Preparation time **20 minutes**
Cooking time **30–35 minutes**

4 fresh **artichokes**
3 tablespoons **olive oil**, plus
    extra for drizzling (optional)
1 **shallot**, finely chopped
1 **garlic clove**, crushed
75 g (3 oz) **fresh white
    breadcrumbs**
finely grated rind of ½ **lemon**
handful of **parsley**, chopped
squeeze of **lemon juice**
salt and **pepper**

Prepare the artichokes by cutting off the bases so that they can lie flat, then trim off the top 2 cm (¾ inch) of each artichoke. Using kitchen scissors, snip away any spikes on the leaves. Cook the artichokes in a saucepan of boiling water for 20 minutes or until you can easily pull away one of the leaves.

Meanwhile, heat the oil in a frying pan, add the shallot and cook for 3 minutes until softened. Stir in the garlic and cook for a further 30 seconds, then add the breadcrumbs, lemon rind, parsley, salt and pepper and stir to combine. Remove the pan from the heat and set aside.

Drain the artichokes, then cool under cold running water and drain again. Pull away the very pale leaves from the centre of each artichoke, then, using a spoon, scrape around below these leaves to completely remove the hairy choke, ensuring the flesh of the soft heart, which lies just beneath, remains.

Place the artichokes on a lightly greased baking sheet and spoon a little of the breadcrumb mixture into the centre of each. Squeeze over a little lemon juice and drizzle with extra olive oil, if liked. Bake in a preheated oven, 200°C (400°F), Gas Mark 6, for 10–15 minutes until the artichokes are very tender and the breadcrumbs are crisp.

For seared artichokes with lemon, heat 1 tablespoon olive oil in a frying pan, add 150 g (5 oz) thinly sliced ready-cooked artichoke hearts and cook for 2–3 minutes until golden, then add 1 sliced garlic clove and cook for a further 30 seconds. Squeeze over a little lemon juice and serve scattered with parsley.

charred asparagus with manchego

Serves **4**
Preparation time **5 minutes**
Cooking time **3–5 minutes**

250 g (8 oz) **asparagus
spears**, trimmed
1 tablespoon **olive oil**, plus
extra for drizzling
grated rind and juice of
½ **lemon**
25 g (1 oz) **flaked almonds**,
toasted
handful of **Manchego cheese**
shavings
salt and **pepper**

Toss the asparagus in the oil and season well. Heat a
griddle pan until smoking hot, then add the asparagus
and cook for 3–5 minutes, turning frequently, until
tender and lightly charred.

Transfer to a serving plate, then scatter over the lemon
rind and squeeze over the juice. Scatter over the almonds
and Manchego shavings and serve drizzled with a little
extra olive oil.

For scrambled eggs with asparagus & Manchego,
cook 200 g (7 oz) asparagus tips in a saucepan of
boiling water for 3 minutes or until tender. Drain, then
cool under cold running water and drain again. Break
5 eggs into a saucepan and drizzle over 3 tablespoons
olive oil. Cook over a low heat, stirring gently as the
eggs start to set. Add the asparagus and continue
to cook until the eggs are soft and just set and the
asparagus is warmed through. Serve scattered with
a little grated Manchego cheese.

butter bean & potato casserole

Serves **4**
Preparation time **15 minutes**
Cooking time **1 hour**

1 tablespoon **olive oil**
1 mild **Spanish onion**, sliced
2 **garlic cloves**, crushed
200 g (7 oz) **potatoes**, peeled
and diced
65 g (2½ oz) **turnip**, peeled
and thinly sliced
2 x 410 g (13½ oz) cans
butter beans, rinsed and
drained
100 ml (3½ fl oz) **red wine**
400 g (13 oz) can **chopped
tomatoes**
250 ml (8 fl oz) **vegetable
stock**
pinch of **sweet paprika**
1 **bay leaf**
2 tablespoons chopped **flat
leaf parsley**
salt and **pepper**

Pour the oil into a flameproof casserole, add the onion
and cook over a low heat for 10 minutes. Add the garlic,
potatoes, turnip and butter beans and stir to combine.

Add all the remaining ingredients, season with salt
and pepper and bring to a simmer, then cover.

Transfer the casserole to a preheated oven, 180°C
(350°F), Gas Mark 4, and cook for 45 minutes.
Check the seasoning and scatter with the chopped
parsley. Serve with a green salad, if liked.

For butter bean & tomato casserole, make as above,
omitting the potatoes and turnips and using 2 sliced
onions, 3 rinsed and drained 410 g (13½ oz) cans
butter beans and 2 x 400 g (13 oz) cans chopped
tomatoes. Add several oregano sprigs and simmer
on the hob for 15 minutes, rather than in the oven.
Serve warm with crusty bread.

chilled gazpacho

Serves **6**

Preparation time **20 minutes**, plus chilling

875 g (1¾ lb) **tomatoes**

½ **cucumber**, roughly chopped

2 **red peppers**, cored, deseeded and roughly chopped

1 **celery stick**, chopped

2 **garlic cloves**, chopped

½ **red chilli**, deseeded and sliced

small handful of **fresh coriander** or **flat leaf parsley**, plus extra to garnish

2 tablespoons **white wine vinegar**

2 tablespoons **sun-dried tomato paste**

4 tablespoons **olive oil**

salt

To serve

ice cubes

hard-boiled egg, finely chopped (optional)

cucumber, red pepper and **onion**, finely chopped (optional)

Place the tomatoes in a heatproof bowl and pour over boiling water to cover. Leave for 1–2 minutes, then drain, cut a cross at the stem end of each tomato and peel off the skins. Roughly chop.

Mix the tomatoes with the vegetables, garlic, chilli and coriander or parsley in a large bowl. Add the vinegar, tomato paste, oil and a little salt. Process in batches in a food processor or blender until smooth, scraping the mixture down from the sides of the bowl if necessary.

Collect the blended mixtures together in a clean bowl and check the seasoning, adding a little more salt if needed. Cover and chill for up to 24 hours.

Ladle the gazpacho into large bowls, scatter with ice cubes and a little finely chopped hard-boiled egg, cucumber, pepper and onion, if liked, then garnish with chopped coriander or parsley.

potato & onion tortilla

Serves **6**
Preparation time **10 minutes**
Cooking time **30 minutes**

750 g (1 ½ lb) **baking
potatoes**, peeled and very
thinly sliced
4 tablespoons **olive oil**
2 large **onions**, thinly sliced
6 **eggs**, beaten
salt and **pepper**

Place the potato slices in a bowl and toss with a
little salt and pepper. Heat the oil in a medium-sized,
heavy-based frying pan, add the potatoes and fry very
gently for 10 minutes, turning frequently, until softened
but not browned.

Add the onions and fry gently for a further 5 minutes
without browning. Spread the potatoes and onions in
an even layer in the pan and reduce the heat as low
as possible.

Pour over the eggs, cover and cook very gently for
about 15 minutes until the eggs have set. (If the
centre of the omelette is too wet, put the pan under a
preheated medium grill to finish cooking.) Tip the tortilla
on to a plate and serve warm or cold with a mixed salad.

crispy aubergine with honey

Serves **4**
Preparation time **10 minutes**,
  plus standing
Cooking time **10 minutes**

1 teaspoon **salt**
1 large **aubergine**, sliced
125 g (4 oz) **plain flour**
vegetable oil, for deep-frying
4 tablespoons **clear honey**

Sprinkle the salt over the aubergine in a colander and leave to stand for 20 minutes. Pat dry with kitchen paper.

Place the flour on a plate, then dip the aubergine slices in the flour until well coated.

Pour the oil into a large, deep saucepan or deep-fat fryer to a depth of at least 7 cm (3 inches) and heat to 180–190°C (350–375°F), or until a cube of bread browns in 30 seconds. Deep-fry the aubergine slices in batches for 3 minutes until crispy and golden, then remove with a slotted spoon. Drain on kitchen paper and keep warm while you cook the remaining slices.

Transfer the slices to a serving plate, drizzle over the honey and serve warm.

For roasted aubergine with spicy honey dressing, Cut 2 aubergines into chunks. Toss together with 2 tablespoons olive oil, season with salt and pepper and spread out in a roasting tray. Roast in a preheated oven, 200°C (400°F), Gas Mark 6, for 20 minutes, turning once, until soft and golden. Leave to cool a little. Whisk together 1 teaspoon white wine vinegar, 2 teaspoons clear honey, ½ red chilli, deseeded and chopped, and 3 tablespoons extra virgin olive oil. Toss together with the warm aubergine and sprinkle over chopped mint leaves to serve.

paprika & caper cauliflower

Serves **4–6**
Preparation time **5 minutes**
Cooking time **25 minutes**

1 head of **cauliflower**, broken
  into florets
3 tablespoons **olive oil**
½ teaspoon **hot smoked
  paprika**
2 teaspoons **capers**, drained
salt and **pepper**

Toss together the cauliflower, oil and paprika in a
bowl, then season. Place in a shallow baking dish
and roast in a preheated oven, 220°C (425°F),
Gas Mark 7, for 20 minutes, shaking the dish
occasionally during cooking.

Scatter over the capers, return to the oven and
cook for a further 5 minutes or until the cauliflower
is tender and charred.

For cauliflower, red pepper & caper salad, roast the
cauliflower as above and leave to cool. Whisk together
1 ½ tablespoons lemon juice, ½ red chilli, deseeded and
chopped, and 3 tablespoons extra virgin olive oil and
season well. Arrange the cauliflower and 2 drained and
sliced ready-roasted red peppers from a jar on a serving
plate. Drizzle over the dressing, then scatter with the
drained capers.

roasted stuffed peppers

Serves **2**
Preparation time **10 minutes**
Cooking time **1 hour**

4 large **red peppers**, halved
   lengthways, cored and
   deseeded
2 **garlic cloves**, crushed
1 tablespoon chopped **thyme**,
   plus extra to garnish
4 **plum tomatoes**, halved
4 tablespoons **extra virgin
   olive oil**
2 tablespoons **balsamic
   vinegar**
salt and **pepper**

Place the pepper halves, cut-sides up, in an ovenproof dish or a roasting tin lined with foil. Divide the garlic and thyme between them and season with salt and pepper.

Put a tomato half in each pepper and drizzle with the oil and vinegar. Roast in a preheated oven, 220°C (425°F), Gas Mark 7, for 55 minutes–1 hour until the peppers are soft and charred.

Serve with some crusty bread to mop up the juices and a baby leaf salad, if liked.

desserts

seville orange & chocolate tart

Serves **8–10**
Preparation time **20 minutes**,
 plus chilling and cooling
Cooking time **35–40 minutes**

200 g (7 oz) **plain dark
 chocolate**, broken into
 pieces
100 g (3½ oz) **butter**
2 **eggs**
2 **egg yolks**
75 g (3 oz) **caster sugar**
4 tablespoons **fine-cut Seville
 orange marmalade**
sliced **crystallized orange**,
 to decorate

Pastry
50 g (2 oz) **icing sugar**
250 g (8 oz) **plain flour**
125 g (4 oz) cold **butter**,
 cubed
1 **egg**, beaten
finely grated rind of 1 **orange**
pinch of **salt**

Make the pastry. Place the icing sugar and flour in a bowl, add the butter and rub in with your fingertips until the mixture resembles fine breadcrumbs. Add the egg, orange rind and salt and mix to a soft dough. Wrap in clingfilm and chill for 20 minutes.

Roll out the pastry on a lightly floured work surface and use to line a 23 cm (9 inch) tart tin. Chill for 30 minutes. Trim off the excess pastry, then line the tart with baking paper and fill with baking beans. Bake in a preheated oven, 200°C (400°F), Gas Mark 6, for 10 minutes. Remove the paper and beans, then cook for a further 10 minutes until crisp and golden. Leave to cool. Reduce the oven temperature to 180°C (350°F), Gas Mark 4.

Melt the chocolate and butter in a heatproof bowl set over a small pan of simmering water, making sure the water does not touch the surface of the bowl. Leave to cool slightly. Beat the eggs, egg yolks and sugar in a bowl until light and fluffy, then stir in the cooled chocolate mix.

Spread the marmalade over the tart, then pour in the chocolate mixture. Bake in the oven for 15–20 minutes until just set. Leave to cool, then decorate with sliced Crystallized Orange (see below). Serve with crème fraîche.

For homemade crystallized orange, remove the peel of 1 orange with a sharp knife. Discard any pith, cut into thick strips and cook in a small saucepan of boiling water for 20 minutes until softened. Drain. Heat 150 ml (¼ pint) water and 100 g (3½ oz) caster sugar in a saucepan until the sugar has dissolved. Add the peel and cook gently for 20 minutes until syrupy. Remove the peel and dip in granulated sugar until well covered, then leave to dry on a wire rack in a cool, dry place.

wine & honey-baked figs

Serves **4**
Preparation time **5 minutes**
Cooking time **15–20 minutes**

250 ml (8 fl oz) **fruity red
   wine**, such as Rioja
3 tablespoons **soft brown
   sugar**
3 tablespoons **clear honey**
1 **cinnamon stick**
12 small **figs**
25 g (1 oz) **butter**

Place the wine, sugar, honey and cinnamon stick in a saucepan and simmer until the sugar has dissolved. Cut a small cross down into the top of each fig using a sharp knife, then place in a greased baking dish. Pour the wine mixture over each fig and top each with a little of the butter.

Bake in a preheated oven, 200°C (400°F), Gas Mark 6, for 10–15 minutes until the figs are soft. Serve with yogurt or crème fraîche and the sauce drizzled over.

For fig & orange salad with red wine syrup, place the wine as above and 200 g (7 oz) caster sugar in a small saucepan and cook until the sugar has dissolved and is slightly syrupy. Leave to cool. Mix together 8 sliced figs and 2 peeled and sliced oranges and arrange on a serving plate. Drizzle with the wine syrup and serve with vanilla ice cream.

almond & lemon meringues

Serves **4–6**
Preparation time **20 minutes**
Cooking time **1¼ hours**

4 egg whites
125 g (4 oz) **caster sugar**
125 g (4 oz) **icing sugar**
finely grated rind of **1 lemon**
25 g (1 oz) **flaked almonds**

Whisk the egg whites in a large, clean bowl until stiff peaks form. Gradually whisk in the caster sugar, a spoonful at a time, until stiff and glossy. Whisk in the icing sugar, in 3 batches, until the meringue is stiff and resembles shaving foam. Fold in the lemon rind.

Spoon 15–16 small mounds of the meringue on to 2 baking sheets lined with baking paper, leaving space between each one. Sprinkle the almonds over the tops.

Bake in a preheated oven, 110°C (225°F), Gas Mark ¼, for 1¼ hours until crisp and dry and the meringues sound hollow when tapped on the bottom. Leave to cool before serving.

For meringues with chocolate sauce, make the meringues as above. When cool, pile the meringues up on a plate. Heat 125 ml (4 fl oz) double cream in a small saucepan until boiling. Place 125 g (4 oz) chopped plain dark chocolate in a heatproof bowl, pour over the hot cream and stir until smooth. Drizzle the warm sauce over the meringues and serve.

sherry & raisin ice cream

Serves **8**

Preparation time **15 minutes**, plus soaking, cooling and freezing

Cooking time **10 minutes**

100 g (3½ oz) **raisins**, preferably Malaga

100 ml (3½ fl oz) **sweet sherry**, preferably Pedro Ximenez, plus extra to serve (optional)

300 ml (½ pint) **milk**

600 ml (1 pint) **double cream**

1 teaspoon **vanilla extract**

6 **egg yolks**

125 g (4 oz) **caster sugar**

Tip the raisins into a bowl and pour over the sherry, then leave to soak for 1 hour.

Heat the milk, cream and vanilla extract in a saucepan until almost boiling. Meanwhile, beat together the egg yolks and sugar in a heatproof bowl until pale and thickened. Stir in a spoonful of the hot cream mixture, then pour the egg mixture into the pan and cook over a low heat, stirring frequently, until it coats the back of a wooden spoon, making sure it doesn't boil. Remove the pan from the heat, cover the surface of the custard with clingfilm and leave to cool.

Place the custard in an ice-cream maker and churn until frozen following the manufacturer's instructions, adding the raisin mixture just before the ice cream is ready. Alternatively, freeze the custard in a shallow freezerproof container until almost solid, then beat until smooth and return to the freezer. Repeat this 2 more times, stirring in the sherry and raisin mixture after the final beating. Freeze until solid.

Serve scoops of ice cream drizzled with extra sherry or Caramel, Sherry & Raisin Sauce (see below), if liked.

For caramel, sherry & raisin sauce, to serve as an accompaniment, place 100 g (3½ oz) caster sugar and 100 ml (3½ fl oz) water in a saucepan and cook until the sugar has dissolved and the mixture is a golden brown colour. Remove the pan from the heat and stir in 50 ml (2 fl oz) each of sweet sherry, preferably Pedro Ximenez, and water. Return to the heat to dissolve any hardened caramel. Stir in 75 g (3 oz) raisins and leave to cool slightly before serving.

santiago almond torte

Serves **8**

Preparation time **15 minutes**, plus cooling

Cooking time **45–50 minutes**

300 g (10 oz) **blanched almonds**
5 **eggs**, separated
250 g (8 oz) **caster sugar**
finely grated rind of 1 **lemon**
finely grated rind of 1 **orange**
1 teaspoon **ground cinnamon**
icing sugar, for dusting
créme fraîche, to serve

Place the almonds in large, dry frying pan over a low heat and toast for 5–10 minutes, shaking the pan frequently, until lightly browned. Leave to cool, then tip into a food processor and pulse until finely ground.

Beat the egg yolks in a bowl until pale and thickened, then beat in the sugar, citrus rind and cinnamon. Stir in the ground almonds.

Whisk the egg whites in a large, clean bowl until stiff peaks form. Stir one-third into the almond mixture to loosen, then gently fold in the remaining mixture in 2 batches. Spoon the mixture into a greased and base-lined 23 cm (9 inch) springform cake tin.

Bake in a preheated oven, 180°C (350°F), Gas Mark 4, for 40 minutes or until the sides start to shrink away from the tin. Leave to cool in the tin for 10 minutes, then turn out on to a wire rack and leave to cool. Dust with icing sugar, cut into slices and serve with crème fraîche.

For almond torte with citrus glaze, make the cake as above. Meanwhile, place 25 g (1 oz) caster sugar, the pared rind of ½ orange, the juice and pared rind of 1 lemon and 2 tablespoons water in a saucepan and cook over a low heat until the sugar has dissolved. Set aside. Remove the cake from the oven and pierce the top with a metal skewer. Remove the rind from the citrus glaze, then pour over the cake and leave to cool.

chocolate pots with churros

Serves **6**

Preparation time **20 minutes**,
 plus chilling and resting

Cooking time **25 minutes**

75 g (3 oz) **granulated sugar**
3 tablespoons **cornflour**
25 g (1 oz) **cocoa powder**
3 **eggs**
500 ml (17 fl oz) **milk**
75 g (3 oz) **milk chocolate**,
 chopped

Churros
125 g (4 oz) **plain flour**
125 g (4 oz) **self-raising flour**
25 g (1 oz) **butter**, melted
450 ml (¾ pint) **boiling water**
vegetable oil, for deep-frying
75 g (3 oz) **caster sugar**

Beat together the granulated sugar, cornflour, cocoa powder and eggs in a heatproof bowl. Heat the milk until boiling, then whisk into the egg mixture. Pour the mixture into a pan and cook for 3–5 minutes until thickened, making sure it doesn't boil. Pour the hot custard over the chocolate in a heatproof bowl and stir until smooth. Cover and chill for at least 1 hour.

Make the churros. Sift the flours into a bowl and make a well in the centre. Mix together the melted butter and measurement water in a jug, then pour into the well, beating to form a smooth dough. Leave to rest for 10 minutes.

Pour the oil into a large, deep saucepan to a depth of at least 7 cm (3 inches) and heat to 180–190°C (350–375°F), or until a cube of bread browns in 30 seconds. Spoon the dough into a piping bag, then squeeze 5 cm (2 inch) lengths into the oil, cutting off the ends with scissors – only cook 5 at a time. Deep-fry for about 3 minutes until golden, then remove with a slotted spoon. Drain on kitchen paper and keep warm while you cook the remaining dough. Sprinkle the churros with the caster sugar. Serve the warm churros with the chocolate custard in small serving dishes on the side for dunking.

For rich hot chocolate with churros, make the churros as above. Mix 2 teaspoons cornflour with 2 tablespoons milk. Heat 500 ml (17 fl oz) milk and 300 ml (½ pint) single cream in a saucepan until just boiling. Stir in the cornflour mixture and cook for 1 minute until slightly thickened. Divide 200 g (7 oz) finely chopped plain dark chocolate between 6 serving cups. Pour over the hot milk and stir until melted, adding sugar to taste. Serve with the warm churros.

custard tart with cherry sauce

Serves **8**

Preparation time **30 minutes**, plus cooling

Cooking time **1 hour–1 hour 20 minutes**

500 g (1 lb) pack **puff pastry**

300 ml (½ pint) **milk**

300 ml (½ pint) **double cream**

pared rind of ½ **lemon**, cut into strips

1 **vanilla pod**, split in half lengthways

2 **eggs**

4 **egg yolks**

125 g (4 oz) **caster sugar**

Cherry sauce

200 g (7 oz) **morello cherry conserve**

1 tablespoon **aniseed liqueur**, such as Pernod (optional)

Roll out the pastry on a lightly floured work surface and use to line a 23 cm (9 inch) tart tin, allowing a little overhang. Prick the base with a fork and line with baking paper. Place a 20 cm (8 inch) cake tin in the case, then fill with baking beans. Cook in a preheated oven, 200°C (400°F), Gas Mark 6, for 20–25 minutes until the sides are set. Remove the inner tin and paper. Return to the oven and cook for a further 10–15 minutes until golden and crisp. Press down any risen bits, then leave to cool. Trim any excess pastry.

Place the milk, cream and lemon rind in a saucepan and scrape in the seeds from the vanilla pod. Simmer for 5 minutes. Beat the eggs, egg yolks and sugar in a bowl until pale and thickened. Stir in a spoonful of the hot cream, then pour the egg mixture into the pan and cook over a low heat for 5–10 minutes, stirring frequently, until it coats the back of a spoon. Leave to cool slightly.

Strain the mixture through a sieve and pour into the pastry case. Bake in a preheated oven, 180°C (350°F), Gas Mark 4, for 20–25 minutes until firm with just a slight wobble in the centre. Leave to cool.

Stir together the cherry conserve and liqueur, if using. Drizzle over the custard tart to serve.

For cherry creams, heat 600 ml (1 pint) each of milk, and double cream, 125 g (4 oz) caster sugar and the seeds of 1 vanilla pod in a saucepan until boiling. Meanwhile, cover 8 gelatine leaves with cold water and leave to soften for 5 minutes. Remove the pan from the heat and stir in the gelatine until dissolved. Pour into 8 ramekins and chill overnight. Make the cherry sauce as above and spoon over the creams to serve.

creamy rice pudding

Serves **4–6**
Preparation time **5 minutes**
Cooking time **50 minutes**

1 litre (1¾ pints) **milk**
250 ml (8 fl oz) **double cream**
100 g (3½ oz) **caster sugar**
1 **cinnamon stick**
pared rind of ½ **lemon**, cut
  into strips
200 g (7 oz) **pudding** or
  risotto rice
2 **egg yolks**, beaten
ground cinnamon, for
  sprinkling (optional)

Place the milk, cream, sugar, cinnamon stick and lemon rind in a large saucepan and bring to the boil. Add the rice, stir well and reduce the heat to low. Cook for 45 minutes, stirring occasionally, until most of the liquid has been absorbed and the rice is very tender.

Stir a spoonful of the liquid into the beaten egg yolks, then pour the egg mixture into the pan and cook for a further 1 minute until the pudding is creamy. Remove the cinnamon stick and lemon rind. Serve warm or chilled, sprinkled with a little ground cinnamon, if liked.

For caramelized rice puddings, make the rice pudding as above. Spoon into 4 ramekins and leave to cool slightly. Sprinkle 1 tablespoon caster sugar over the top of each pudding, making sure the tops are covered. Caramelize the tops using a blowtorch or place under a preheated hot grill for 1–2 minutes until the sugar browns and melts.

orange caramel flan

Serves **4**

Preparation time **15 minutes**,
  plus cooling and chilling

Cooking time **35 minutes**

finely grated rind and juice of
  5 large **oranges**
250 g (8 oz) **caster sugar**
1 tablespoon **cornflour**
6 **eggs**
3 **egg yolks**

Caramel
75 g (3 oz) **caster sugar**
5 tablespoons **water**

Make the caramel. Place the sugar and measurement water in a saucepan and cook over a low heat until the sugar has dissolved. Increase the heat and cook until it is a caramel colour. Divide between 4 dariole moulds, coating the bases and a little up the sides.

Place the orange rind, 400 ml (14 fl oz) of the orange juice and the sugar in a saucepan and cook over a low heat until the sugar has dissolved. Mix the cornflour with 2 tablespoons of the remaining orange juice (or water), then stir into the pan and cook for 2 minutes until thickened. Pass through a fine sieve and leave to cool slightly.

Beat the eggs and egg yolks in a large bowl, then stir in the orange mixture, a little at a time. Spoon into the prepared moulds, place in a roasting tin and pour in boiling water to come two-thirds up the sides of the moulds. Bake in a preheated oven, 150°C (300°F), Gas Mark 2, for 20–25 minutes until just set with a slight wobble in the centres.

Leave to cool, then chill for at least 2 hours or overnight. Turn out on to serving plates and serve.

For creamy orange flan, whisk 125 g (4 oz) caster sugar, 4 eggs, 6 egg yolks, 250 ml (8 fl oz) each of orange juice and double cream and 1 teaspoon finely grated orange rind in a large bowl. Pour into a 20 cm (8 inch) greased pie dish or springform cake tin. Place in a deep roasting tin with boiling water as above. Bake in a preheated oven, 160°C (325°F), Gas Mark 3, for 1¼–1½ hours until just set. Leave to cool, then turn out on to a serving plate and serve with fresh oranges.

lemon sorbet

Serves **4**

Preparation time **20 minutes**,
  plus cooling and freezing

Cooking time **5 minutes**

6 lemons

250 g (8 oz) **caster sugar**

375 ml (13 fl oz) **water**

2 **egg whites**

Remove the rind from 2 of the lemons using a vegetable peeler and squeeze the juice into a bowl. Set aside the juice and place the rind in a saucepan with the sugar. Pour in the measurement water and cook until the sugar has dissolved. Leave to cool.

Trim one end of the 4 remaining lemons so that they stand upright, then cut off the tops. Scoop out the flesh and squeeze the juice into the reserved lemon juice. Place the lemon shells in the freezer.

Add all the lemon juice to the cooled sugar syrup, then pass through a sieve. Place the syrup in an ice-cream machine and churn following the manufacturer's instructions.

When the sorbet is almost frozen, whisk the egg whites in a clean bowl until soft peaks form. Transfer the sorbet to a bowl and beat, then stir in one-third of the whisked egg whites. Gradually stir in the remaining whites in 2 batches. Spoon the mixture into the prepared lemon shells and place in the freezer until frozen.

For lemon curd & meringue ice cream, swirl 125 ml (4 fl oz) lemon curd through 500 ml (17 fl oz) softened vanilla ice cream. Crumble over 2 ready-made meringues and return to the freezer until firm.

turrón parfait

Serves **10–12**
Preparation time **20 minutes**,
    plus cooling and freezing
Cooking time **5 minutes**

2 **egg whites**
75 g (3 oz) **caster sugar**
300 ml (½ pint) **double cream**
2 tablespoons **clear honey**

Nut brittle
150 g (5 oz) **caster sugar**
1 tablespoon **water**
50 g (2 oz) **blanched
    hazelnuts**, toasted
50 g (2 oz) **blanched
    almonds**, toasted

Make the nut brittle. Place the sugar and measurement water in a saucepan and cook over a low heat until the sugar has dissolved, then increase the heat and continue to cook until the mixture is a golden caramel colour. Place the nuts close together on a baking sheet lined with baking paper. Pour over the caramel, then leave to cool until completely set and hard. Smash up the nuts with a rolling pin and then, reserving a few big pieces for decoration, place the remainder in a food processor and pulse until mostly broken up.

Whisk the egg whites in a clean bowl until stiff peaks form. Gradually whisk in the sugar, a spoonful at a time, until stiff and glossy. In a separate bowl, whip the cream until it just holds its shape. Gently fold the meringue into the cream in 3 batches. Stir in the honey and pulsed nuts. Spoon the mixture into a 1.2 litre (2 pint) loaf tin lined with clingfilm and smooth the top. Place in the freezer overnight until firm.

Transfer the parfait to the refrigerator and leave to soften for 10 minutes. Turn out on to a plate, scatter over the reserved nut brittle and serve cut into slices.

For easy turrón ice cream with chocolate sauce,
place 200 g (7 oz) shop-bought turrón or nougat in a food processor and pulse until broken into small pieces, then stir through 500 ml (17 fl oz) softened vanilla ice cream and transfer to a freezerproof container. Cover with clingfilm and freeze until firm. Heat 150 ml (¼ pint) double cream in a saucepan until boiling. Place 150 g (5 oz) chopped dark chocolate in a heatproof bowl, pour over the hot cream and stir until smooth. Serve scoops of the ice cream drizzled with the chocolate sauce.

moscatel roasted peaches

Serves **6**
Preparation time **10 minutes**
Cooking time **25–30 minutes**

6 ripe **peaches**
250 ml (8 fl oz) **moscatel** or
    other **sweet wine**
75 ml (3 fl oz) **water**
1 **vanilla pod**, split lengthways
thick strip of **lemon rind**
1 **cinnamon stick**
4 tablespoons **clear honey**
25 g (1 oz) shelled **pistachio
    nuts**, chopped
créme fraîche or **natural
    yogurt**, to serve

Place the peaches in a large baking dish. Pour over
the wine and measurement water, then add the vanilla
pod, lemon rind and cinnamon stick. Drizzle over the
honey and bake in a preheated oven, 190°C (375°F),
Gas Mark 5, for 25–30 minutes until the peaches
are tender.

Scatter over the pistachios and serve with the juices
and crème fraîche or natural yogurt.

For marinated peaches, pour boiling water over the
peaches, then peel off the skins. Halve, stone and slice
the peaches, then place in a shallow dish. Pour in 200 ml
(7 fl oz) moscatel or other sweet wine and sprinkle over
2–3 tablespoons caster sugar to taste. Chill for at least
3 hours. Serve with dollops of natural yogurt.

catalan cream puddings

Serves **6**

Preparation time **15 minutes**,
  plus infusing and cooling

Cooking time **40 minutes**

300 ml (½ pint) **double cream**

300 ml (½ pint) **milk**

pared rind of 1 **lemon**, cut into
  strips

1 **cinnamon stick**

6 **egg yolks**

100 g (3½ oz) **caster sugar**,
  plus extra for sprinkling

Place the cream, milk, lemon rind and cinnamon stick in a saucepan and bring to the boil. Remove from the heat and leave to infuse for 30 minutes. Beat together the egg yolks and sugar in a bowl, then gradually whisk in the warm cream mixture.

Put 6 ramekins in a deep roasting tin and pour in boiling water to come halfway up the sides of the ramekins. Pass the custard through a fine sieve into a measuring jug, discarding the cinnamon and lemon rind, then pour into the ramekins. Bake in a preheated oven, 180°C (350°F), Gas Mark 4, for 30 minutes until just set with a slight wobble in the centres. Remove from the tin and leave to cool completely in the refrigerator.

When ready to serve, sprinkle over enough sugar to cover the tops of the custards. Caramelize the tops using a blowtorch or place under a preheated hot grill for 1–2 minutes until the sugar browns and melts.

For caramel orange creams, place 125 g (4 oz) caster sugar and 50 ml (2 fl oz) water in a small saucepan and cook until the sugar has dissolved, then increase the heat and continue to cook until the mixture is a golden caramel colour. Pour the caramel into the bottom of 6 ramekins and leave to harden. Make the pudding mixture as above, replacing the pared lemon rind with the finely grated rind of 2 oranges and omitting the cinnamon stick. Pour into the ramekins and bake as above. Chill overnight, then turn out on to serving plates, drizzling the caramel sauce over.

raisin toasts with sherry cream

Serves **6**

Preparation time **15 minutes**,
  plus soaking

Cooking time **15 minutes**

3 **eggs**

1 **egg yolk**

125 ml (4 fl oz) **single cream**

125 ml (4 fl oz) **sweet sherry**

6 thick slices of **raisin bread**,
  halved

50 g (2 oz) **butter**

2 tablespoons **caster sugar**

300 ml (½ pint) **double cream**

6 tablespoons **clear honey**

Beat together the eggs, egg yolk, single cream and 2 tablespoons of the sherry in a bowl. Transfer to a shallow bowl, then dip in the bread slices until they have absorbed the liquid and are soft.

Melt a little of the butter in a nonstick frying pan, add the bread in batches and cook for about 5 minutes, turning once. Remove from the pan and keep warm while you cook the remaining slices.

Stir together the remaining sherry and sugar in a bowl until the sugar has dissolved. Add the double cream and whip until soft peaks form.

Place the toast on serving plates. Serve with dollops of the sherry cream drizzled with the honey.

For sherry & raisin bread pudding, heat 150 ml (¼ pint) sweet sherry and 125 g (4 oz) raisins in a saucepan until just boiling, then leave to stand for 2 hours. Heat 300 ml (½ pint) each of double cream and milk in a saucepan until boiling. Beat together 3 eggs, 100 g (3½ oz) caster sugar and 1 teaspoon vanilla extract in a heatproof bowl until smooth, then slowly whisk in the hot cream mixture. Butter 6 slices of brioche bread, then cut and fit into a greased medium-sized baking dish. Pour over the raisins and sherry, then the custard and leave to stand for 15 minutes. Bake in a preheated oven, 180°C (350°F), Gas Mark 4, for 40 minutes until just set.

index

acknowledgements

Commissioning editor: Eleanor Maxfield
Senior editor: Sybella Stephens
Text editor: Jo Murray
Art direction and design: Penny Stock
Photographer: William Shaw
Home economist: Emma Lewis
Prop stylist: Liz Hippisley
Production controller: Sarah Kramer